A Christian Approach to Careers

Life Planning

Kirk E. Farnsworth
& Wendell H. Lawhead

A workbook for those beginning to look for a job
and those seeking a change in midlife.

InterVarsity Press
Downers Grove
Illinois 60515

InterVarsity Press is the book-publishing division of Inter-Varsity Christian Fellowship, a student movement active on campus at hundreds of universities, colleges and schools of nursing. For information about local and regional activities, write IVCF, 233 Langdon St., Madison, WI 53703.

Distributed in Canada through InterVarsity Press, 1875 Leslie St., Unit 10, Don Mills, Ontario M3B 2M5, Canada.

ISBN 0-87784-840-8

Printed in the United States of America

20	19	18	17	16	15	14	13	12	11	10	9	8	7	6	5	4	3	2	1
98	97	96	95	94	93	92	91	90	89	88	87	86	85	84	83	82	81		

TABLE OF CONTENTS

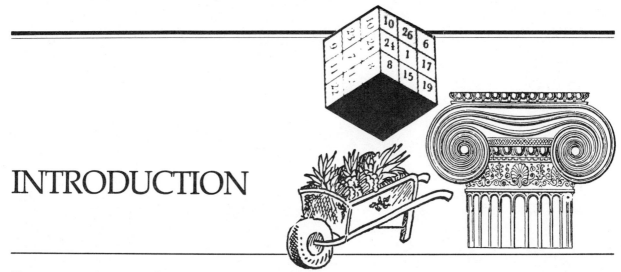

INTRODUCTION

Do you wonder what God has in store for you? Do you want to do his will, but just can't decide what that is? Or are you troubled with career-related pressures, such as conflicting advice about what is good for you and what you are good for, or conflicting vocational opportunities which seem to be controlled by society's whims, or conflicting ideas about yourself?

Perhaps you are struggling with an internal dialog between the sacred and the secular, that runs something like this:

"What does it profit a man, to gain the whole world and forfeit his life?" (Mk. 8:36).

"How do you expect to get ahead if you're not majoring in something that will earn you a bundle when you graduate?"

"If any one will not work, let him not eat" (2 Thess. 3:10).

"There's more to life than my job."

"It will be hard for a rich man to enter the kingdom of heaven" (Mt. 19:23).

"Ideals don't pay the rent."

"Do not lay up for yourselves treasures on earth. . . . Where your treasure is, there will your heart be also. . . . No one can serve two masters. . . . You cannot serve God and mammon. . . . Therefore I tell you, do not be anxious about your life, what you shall eat or what you shall drink. . . . But seek first his kingdom and his righteousness, and all these things shall be yours as well" (Mt. 6:19, 21, 24-25, 33).

"If you want to live the good life, you've got to put your career first."

Discovering Yourself

If these are your dilemmas we would like to help you. We would like to be a part of your discovery of who God is creating you to be. We are providing you with a book that will help you uncover your potential, but more importantly, teach you how to discern God's career-related will throughout your life. We see it as essential that what you learn about yourself remain open to further leading from the Lord.

You will be learning specific things about yourself in this book, to be sure, but the main emphasis will be on learning how to learn about yourself throughout your life. Whenever you consider a job change (temporary or permanent), we believe the areas you will work through in this book will apply. Not the answers, necessarily, but the approach.

Another ingredient to life planning that we regard as essential is the context within which career decisions are made. We believe the most fruitful context for you, as a Christian, is that of Christian community. Career decisions can certainly be made anywhere, but learning God's will is going to occur more freely in the company of fellow believers. Throughout this book you will be encouraged to experience self-discovery in the presence of a small group of Christians. This in itself will be important learning for you as you move through the exercises together, giving and receiving feedback. We trust this will also help prepare you to move out into the larger context of the Christian community and, again in the company of believers,

discern your part in the Holy Spirit's plan for equipping the saints.

To lay further groundwork, we suggest you think through the following myths regarding your education, the world of work, sex issues and career planning before your first small group meeting.[1]

Myth #1: College major determines the career of the college graduate.

Myth #2: The college graduate without technical or vocational training has little to offer the world of work.

Myth #3: Every job requires a specific set of abilities and can be prepared for only in a very narrowly circumscribed way.

Myth #4: Since generalists have more difficult times finding and choosing beginning jobs than vocationally specialized graduates, they ultimately end up with low degrees of career stability, satisfaction and success.

Myth #5: Most people begin their careers on graduation and proceed in a straight line toward their ultimate career objectives.

Myth #6: Women would not work if economic reasons did not force them into the labor market.

Myth #7: The employment of mothers leads to juvenile delinquency.

Myth #8: Women are more content than men with intellectually undemanding jobs.

Myth #9: At comparable jobs, women have a higher rate of turnover than men.

Myth #10: Career choice happens once, whether planned or unplanned, and is irreversible from then on.

Actually, many jobs are less specialized than you might think, allowing you considerable freedom to match your unique values, abilities and interests to a variety of vocations. If you are broadly educated, your flexibility will in fact be much greater than for many others because you will have been educated to think and communicate with clarity, to bring an interdisciplinary approach to problem solving and to recognize the need for a human, process orientation in a technologically product-oriented world.

Another asset you potentially have is that if you continue to build on the diversity of your education by gaining exposure to a variety of specific jobs, you will be in a position to coordinate, redirect, and/or combine the diverse talents of a number of other workers. This will be a valuable quality on the job market. The combination of the flexibility of your formal education and the generality of your knowledge of what people do will give you many problem-solving job options in a variety of settings, ranging from industry to education to the church.

Now, if you are smart, what will you do? Perhaps you will start looking at your career more creatively. You will start looking for unmet needs and unsolved problems—for potential jobs—opening up many new areas for the Lord's leading. Employers will rapidly forget that you may or may not have specific job skills when they see that you can improve the performance of their organization. And remember that it is not your first two or three jobs in and of themselves that are crucial, as much as:

(1) identifying all the things you can do, all the aspects of work climates that you like, all the situations where you would rather work with others or alone, and so on; (2) using each successive job to help you develop your basic values, abilities and interests; and (3) applying your assets to problems to be solved.

There are two final facts to keep in mind: First, your assets will change—be alert to subtle shifts in the direction of your values, the effectiveness of your abilities and the diversity of your interests. Second, regardless of the number of job changes you choose to make, your experience will be cumulative, making you an increasingly qualified person, rather than one who is so narrowly trained that when your area of specialty becomes outmoded, so do you! "Whatever your task, work heartily, as serving the Lord and not men" (Col. 3:23). "In the Lord your labor is not in vain" (1 Cor. 15:58).

An Approach, Not an Answer

The basic distinction we are making is between *doing life planning* and *having a life plan*. The goal of this book is the first. We want to give you an *approach* not an *answer*. We hope to help you develop the skills necessary to continually *plan your life* not hand you a once-and-for-all *plan for your life*. The distinction can further be made as follows:

Life Planning	Life Plan
1. Developing an approach to vocational evaluation, as a lifetime process.	1. Making a vocational choice, once and for all, perhaps based on what is currently "the best field to get into."
2. Including business-related electives in your program of study.	2. Taking only courses related to your major interest.
3. Making yourself generally marketable.	3. Fitting yourself to current job-market trends.
4. Taking jobs to test your perceptions of vocational realities and to expand your experience in various work settings.	4. Taking only those jobs that relate to your chosen career.
5. Taking jobs that allow you to be creative in applying your assets to on-the-job situations.	5. Taking jobs that are available and that optimize comfort and security.
6. The advantage is that as you acquire varied work experience, you will better meet the needs of future job markets: problem-solving skills and flexibility.	6. The advantage is in job-entry, whereby your first job will probably be related to your formal education in some way.

The life-planning orientation of this book hopes to liberate students from what Figler refers to as the "vocational reflex": premature career choice based on insecurity and ignorance, and looking for a job only in the area of one's formal education.[2] A Christian need not feel insecure. The faithful need not be fearful! Nor do you need to be ignorant as to your values, abilities, gifts and interests, or your capacity to risk responding to God's call. You do need to be free to be used by God in the area(s) of his choosing. And you need to be free to respond to changes as the Holy Spirit reveals them to you through the Christian community. The first ten units of this book help you to gather such information and to make some preliminary decisions. The last four units help you apply this information directly to career options and planning.

The group context of the exercises in this book underscores the importance of making personal decisions within the framework of the Christian community. It is important that we seek first the kingdom of God (Mt. 6:33) as our calling, and within the context of the body of believers begin to select those work activities that bring honor and glory to the Lord and further his kingdom. Our "career," then, emerges out of and is committed to our kingdom calling. Our vocational skills are as much a part of our overall stewardship as all else that God gives to us to use to further his purpose. They are not our personal property.

Using This Book

We have found the exercises in this book to be very useful in a classroom setting at the college level. We have also adapted the exercises for naturally formed groups such as Bible study groups or Sunday-school groups of young adults and older adults who could benefit from our approach.

Since *we are emphasizing the importance of Christian community in the life-planning process*, it would be far less profitable for an individual to go through the book alone. If you are alone,

we encourage you to seek out at least one other person who will work through this book with you. Everyone who participates should know ahead of time that not only is "homework" required prior to each group meeting, but so is extensive, personal sharing in each meeting. Those who are unwilling to share themselves in such a setting may decide that this book is not for them. If the members of your group are relatively unfamiliar with each other, we recommend that a teacher, pastor, staff person or any other mature Christian act as your facilitator or resource person.

The role of the facilitator/resource person will be to encourage the group to keep the group moving through the book at a steady pace and to help clarify any points of confusion that the book itself does not address. The facilitator/resource person can help best by:

1. convening the group meetings and insuring that they move along at a comfortable pace;
2. fostering a helpful and caring group atmosphere;
3. giving encouragement or clarification when needed during group discussion;
4. intervening in the group process only when asked or if the dynamics are becoming destructive in some way;
5. working through the Bible study materials ahead of the group to be ready to clarify points of confusion and to provide background information that is pertinent to the progress of the group; and
6. encouraging the group to lead itself as much as possible.

Leadership among the members of the group will change from time to time. Different situations call for different members of the group to be leaders or to exercise their styles of leadership. For example, an *implementer* (doer/potentate) translates general agreements into specific group activities, a *suggester* (thinker/prophet) offers ideas in the agreeing stage, and an *encourager* (feeler/pastor) is supportive in the working-out stage. It will be interesting to see how different group members lead as your group progresses through the book. In general, all of the group members can best help each other by:

1. attending all of the group meetings;
2. keeping up with the group (part of the function of the group exercises is to ensure that each member has worked through the individual exercises correctly and that everyone is moving at the same pace);
3. sharing willingly individual work during the group discussions;
4. listening attentively to each other's responses to the discussion questions;
5. making gentle suggestions, asking penetrating questions and sharing creative insights to enhance the clarity of others' thoughts, the accuracy of their self-perceptions and their willingness to consider new alternatives.

There are a few more suggestions to keep in mind.

First, if you have a large group, divide into smaller groups of approximately five each. People who know each other well should be in the same group, if possible.

Second, when you write out responses to the questions in the individual exercises and group discussions, be specific. For example, it's pretty vague to say, "I like gardening because I like to be outdoors." Instead, you might say, "I like gardening because I enjoy the combination of physical and mental activities. I work easily with my hands, and I am good at planning the crop layout and organizing the division of labor for harvesting."

Third, the length of time devoted to each group session should be determined by the group and vary according to individual and group needs. Generally, the minimum amount of time for each group session will be one hour. With time needed between group sessions for the completion of the individual exercises, the total time span will be approximately twelve weeks. Part of the group process will be to decide how much of the book to complete, and therefore, how much total time to devote to the project. This will depend on how far each group member

must progress to meet his or her own life-planning needs. For most groups, we recommend completing at least the first twelve units. (To complete all fourteen units in twelve weeks, we recommend combining units 4 and 5 and units 6 and 7.)

Fourth, in order to complete part four, "Interests," you will need to see a professional counselor to administer the Strong-Campbell Interest Inventory before you begin part one. This is because there will be a time lag before you receive your results. If you do not have access to a counselor, you can order the inventory, profile report and interpretive report directly from:

Customer Service
NCS/Interpretive Scoring Service
4401 West 76th Street.
Minneapolis, MN 55435
(or call 800/328-6116, toll free).

If neither is an option, we have provided alternative material for you to complete the section.

Finally, we caution you not to assume what you learn about yourself in this book is final. That in itself would tie God's hands. Remember that you are basically learning an approach, not answers, to your lifelong quest within the larger Christian community for God's ongoing, dynamic will for your part in furthering his kingdom.

Notes

[1]Derived from J. E. Crowley, T. E. Levitin and R. P. Quinn, "Seven Deadly Half-truths about Women," *Psychology Today*, (March 1973), pp. 93-96; "Ten Myths about Career Decision Making," in H. E. Figler, *PATH: A Career Workbook for Liberal Arts Students* (Cranston, R. I.: The Carroll Press, 1975), pp. 12-14; and "Dealing with Gatekeepers: Which Is Myth and Which Is Fact?" in N. T. Scholz, J. S. Prince and G. P. Miller, *How to Decide: A Guide for Women* (New York: College Entrance Examination Board, 1975), p. 50.

[2]Figler, *PATH*, p. 34.

UNIT 1/*Commitment*

☐ INDIVIDUAL EXERCISE

Reread the introduction (pp. 5-9) in preparation for your first group meeting.

☐ GROUP DISCUSSION

Purposes
☐ To help group members become better acquainted with each other.
☐ To introduce *Life Planning*, its purposes and the amount of involvement that it requires.
☐ To give group members an opportunity to clarify their expectations.
☐ To encourage group members to commit themselves to each other to work through the entire process.

Discussion
1. Begin with introductions, giving your name, where you live and any goal (big or little) that you have in life. As you proceed, write down each group member's name, noting one or two things about each that you learn in the course of the discussion.

Group Members	Comments
_____	_____
_____	_____
_____	_____
_____	_____
_____	_____
_____	_____
_____	_____

2. Below are five sets of questions. Read one set, asking each person to respond briefly in turn before moving on to the next set.

a. Why do you want to work through *Life Planning?*
What do you expect to get out of this?
How much effort do you believe will be necessary to work through this book?

b. How, if at all, have you experienced acceptance in a group in the past?
How, if at all, were you accepting of others?
How might these experiences help or hinder you in this group?

c. Look at the dialog on page 5. Do you feel any similar tensions? If so, how?
Do you think there is a resolution to the tension? If so, how will you find it? If not, why not?

d. Look at the ten myths listed on page 6. Which of these have you considered to be true? Why did or do you accept them as true?
How have these myths affected your view of your own future?

e. What are the differences between doing life planning and having a life plan (see p. 7)?
What do you see as the goal of this book?
Why do the faithful not have to be fearful?

Summary (someone in the group read aloud)

The goal of this book is to give each of us an approach, not an answer, as we continually plan our lives. We should not expect to have a once-and-for-all plan at the end of the book. The idea is to help us get to know ourselves in a group context. This is to be accomplished in two or possibly three ways: (1) through the individual exercises; (2) through group discussion; (3) through other activities, such as group meals or group recreation.

These will take time, energy, honesty and love. *Time:* It will take one to three hours to work through the individual exercise preceding each group meeting. *Energy:* Each of us will need to participate actively in the group discussions, which will not be threatening but will demand sincere involvement. *Honesty:* Being frank about ourselves and the others in the group will help us help each other. *Love:* To speak "the truth in love" (Eph. 4:15) means that care and sensitivity and a spirit of helpfulness must be added to frankness. Truth alone, without love, is not Christian.

Are we ready to make these kinds of sacrifices of time, energy, honesty and love? Does anyone wish to reconsider whether he or she should be in this group? (Note: Discuss, and then someone lead in a brief prayer of commitment for those group members who wish to dedicate themselves to each other for the duration of the book to the glory of God and for his good purpose.)

Looking Ahead

Decide on when you will meet again. Agree that in the meantime you will work through the individual exercise on pages 12-14. Also, decide if you will be using the Strong-Campbell Interest Inventory, and if so, who will obtain them and have them scored. (Remember, if a professional guidance counselor is not available, you can obtain them and have them scored by mail. See p. 9.)

PART I/VALUES
UNIT 2/Life Values

☐ INDIVIDUAL EXERCISE

"I prefer going to football games rather than the symphony."

"I hope that crook gets what's coming to him."

"Don't you care what your parents think about this?"

Each of these comments reflects certain values. In fact, every aspect of daily living must include consideration of such preferences. *Values are enduring beliefs that certain behaviors and that certain results are preferable to others.*

1. Read the following biblical statements. Express in your own words those enduring beliefs about specific behaviors and principles to live by that you discover.

Matthew 6:25-34

Philippians 4:4-9

Colossians 3:1-17

2. Now read over the following list and check the items that you value highly, that you consider to be ideal for your life:

_____ relaxation

_____ physical fitness

_____ hard work

_____ accomplishing goals

_____ beauty

_____ well-reasoned ideas

_____ helping others who are in pain or need

_____ helping others who are being treated unjustly

_____ owning nice things

_____ creativity

_____ education

_____ humility

_____ relating personally with God

_____ dependability

_____ family

_____ personal peace

_____ honesty

_____ loyalty

_____ church

_____ friendship

_____ justice

_____ expensive foods

_____ fine clothing

_____ humor

_____ relating openly and sensitively with others

_____ being around people with similar values

_____ making my own choices

_____ identifying with a particular group

_____ controlling situations

_____ influencing others

_____ being sought after

_____ being talented at several things

_____ staying close to personal roots

_____ money

_____ security

_____ (others) _____

_____

3. Now (a) select five of the values you just checked which you think best describe you now, (b) note the period of your life you most closely associate with the development of each, and (c) record the people you most closely identify with the development of each value.

a. Five most descriptive values (in any order)	b. The period of life most associated with each	c. The people most associated with each
1.		
2.		
3.		
4.		
5.		

4. In addition to rating values as you have just done, we can often gain important insights by considering the values that are worked out in the activities we find enjoyable or satisfying.

First, list below, under "Enjoyable Activities," ten to fifteen specific things you like to do—anything whatsoever that comes to mind that you find enjoyable. (For example: bike riding, visiting shut-ins, caroling.)

AO	GW	$	S	10	Enjoyable Activities	Values[3]
AO	GW	$	S	10	_____	_____
AO	GW	$	S	10	_____	_____
AO	GW	$	S	10	_____	_____
AO	GW	$	S	10	_____	_____
AO	GW	$	S	10	_____	_____
AO	GW	$	S	10	_____	_____
AO	GW	$	S	10	_____	_____
AO	GW	$	S	10	_____	_____
AO	GW	$	S	10	_____	_____
AO	GW	$	S	10	_____	_____
AO	GW	$	S	10	_____	_____
AO	GW	$	S	10	_____	_____
AO	GW	$	S	10	_____	_____
AO	GW	$	S	10	_____	_____
AO	GW	$	S	10	_____	_____

Next, for each activity listed, circle either *A* (if you do it alone) or *O* (if you do it with others); circle either *G* (if the activity is goal oriented) or *W* (if you do it just because you want to); circle *$* if the activity costs $5 or more; circle *S* if the activity is seasonal (for example: snow skiing or pumpkin carving); finally, circle *10* if you hope the activity will be part of your life ten years from now. Do not fill in the "Values" column until your next group meeting.

□ GROUP DISCUSSION

Purposes
□ To identify some of the life values the Bible advocates.
□ To identify the life values personally held by each group member.

Discussion
1. Before starting, facilitator and group members, reread the definitions of your roles on page 8. Then group members briefly respond to the following questions.
2. How did you state the values expressed in Matthew 6:25-34 (see p. 12)?
  Are material things unimportant according to this passage? Explain.
  How do you cope with anxiety about your future?
  What is your attitude toward financial security and accumulating possessions?
3. How did you state the values expressed in Philippians 4:4-9?
  How can we know what is true, honorable, just and so on?
4. How did you state the values expressed in Colossians 3:1-17?
  What are the things above? on earth?
  Is Paul giving realistic commands here? Explain.
5. Do you feel comfortable with the values expressed in these passages? Why or why not?
6. Now briefly share what you wrote down for question 3 (p. 13). The purpose of questions 3b and 3c is twofold: to help you more deeply appreciate some of your more abiding values; to provide a nonthreatening opportunity for positive self-disclosure. (People we choose to remember tend to represent what we like in ourselves.)
7. Now go back to your list of five values (question 3a, p. 13). Record below the three values, in order of priority, which you think are closest to your personal belief system.

First

Second

Third

(Note: Conclusions within each unit are highlighted by heavy rules and will be used again in units 11-14.)

8. Turn to question 4 (p. 14). As each person shares his or her list of activities, other group members should ask questions. Your goal is to help each other identify what is enjoyed or valued in each activity. Each one can then record in the right-hand column what seems to make most sense for him or her. (You can refer to the values listed on p. 13 to stimulate your thinking.) Ask what a person likes about a particular activity. Different people may do the same thing for different reasons. For example, for one, growing flowers may be important because he or she values *beauty*, while another values the *creativity*, while, for still another, it is valued as a *soothing outdoor activity*. Listen carefully to see what each person is feeling about his or her activities and share your observations.

9. After your values column (p. 14) has been filled in, record below the three values listed which seem to be most important, most central to your life.

1. _____

2. _____

3. _____

How do these compare to the three values you listed above in question 7?

Looking Ahead

After completing each unit, you will record the specially identified conclusions in unit 11. Before your next meeting, list on page 50 this unit's conclusions, the highlighted items from pages 15 and 16. Also, complete the individual exercises on pages 17-21.

Note
[3]This aspect of the exercise is adapted from Figler, *PATH*, p. 68.

PART I/VALUES
UNIT 3/*Work Values*

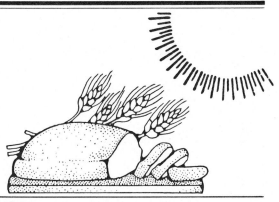

□ INDIVIDUAL EXERCISE

According to Scripture, "There are two things never satisfied, like a leech forever craving more: no, three things! no, four! Hell, the barren womb, a barren desert, fire" (Prov 30:15-16 LB). No, five: people. The Lord says, "The leaders of my people . . . are as greedy as dogs, never satisfied; they . . . only look after their own interest, each trying to get as much as he can for himself from every possible source" (Is. 56:10-11 LB). They can never have enough. How we value work in general and specific work situations is greatly affected by our ability to say, "Enough."

1. Take a look, first, at your most general work values, or what your main purposes are for working. For a biblical perspective, read the manna story in Exodus 16, which took place just after God had miraculously brought Israel out of Egypt across the Red Sea. Then write a brief, personal theology of work. Two important aspects of God's provision to us through work are underscored in Exodus 16: it requires our *obedience* to God; as emphasized by Paul (2 Cor. 8:13-15), it results in our *equality* with each other.

My Understanding of How God Provides through Work

2. To further your understanding of work values in modern society, consider the following laws regarding how God provides through human labor in an agrarian society.[4]

a. The law of gleaning—Deuteronomy 24:19. If you were to abide by this standard today, what values would be appropriate?

Courtesy and generosity

b. The law of limited cropping—Leviticus 25:1-7. If you were to apply this standard today, what values would be appropriate?

c. The law of the first fruits—Deuteronomy 26:10-11. If this standard, what values?

d. The law of interest-free loans—Deuteronomy 23:20. If this standard, what values?

e. The law of tithing—Deuteronomy 14:22-23, 27-29. If this standard, what values?

3. Now let's take a look at how you value specific work activities. Respond to the list of personal-activity work values below[5] with a short phrase or one-sentence response, indicating if you would or would not like each value included in your future jobs and explaining how you view these in work situations.

Work Value (Temperament code)
Example: Variety of duties (1)

I would not like a variety of duties because I like to focus on one main activity over a period of time.

Variety of duties (1)

Repetitive operations (2)

Specific instructions (3)

Planning an entire activity (4)

In-depth interaction with people (5)

Working alone (6)

Influencing others' opinions (7)

Performing well under stress (8)

Using all five senses to make judgments (9)

Comparing products and/or performance against tables/measurements (0)

Creative expression/interpretation (X)

Attaining precise standards (Y)

Frequent change (1)

Standard procedures or sequences (2)

Minimal or no problem solving (3)

Directing activities of others (4)

Interaction beyond giving or receiving instructions (5)

Physical isolation from others (6)

Input into others' attitudes or ideas (7)

Taking risks (8)

Using good judgment (9)

Making contrasts by using verifiable criteria (0)

4. List in any order five of the above work values which are most important to you. (Record the appropriate temperament codes that appear in parentheses following each value. We will consider their significance later in unit eleven.)

Work Value   **(Temperament Code)**

1. _____   (   )

2. _____   (   )

3. _____   (   )

4. _____   (   )

5. _____   (   )

5. Now read through the five pairs of work situations listed below.[6] Indicate your preference for one item in each pair by circling its number. Choosing one statement of work activities or experience implies the rejection of opposite types of activities or experiences. Remember, one item in each pair is not "better" or "worse" than the other. You are only trying to identify your current preferences. Use the insights into your values you gained in question 3 to make your decisions. Although your choices will not be discussed in your next group meeting, they will be taken up in unit eleven. But this is still the best time to work through the pairs.

1 Activities dealing with things and objects.	**Pair I** vs.	**6** Activities concerned with people and the communication of ideas.
2 Activities involving business contacts with people.	**Pair II** vs.	**7** Activities of a scientific and technical nature.
3 Activities of a routine, concrete, organized nature.	**Pair III** vs.	**8** Activities of an abstract and creative nature.
4 Working for people for their presumed good (in the sense of social welfare) or dealing with people in social situations.	**Pair IV** vs.	**9** Activities that are nonsocial in nature and are carried on in relation to processes, machines and techniques.
5 Activities resulting in prestige or in the esteem of others.	**Pair V** vs.	**0** Activities resulting in tangible results or productive satisfaction.

☐ GROUP DISCUSSION

Purposes
☐ To identify a biblical perspective on the value of work.
☐ To identify the work values each group member has regarding specific work situations.

Discussion
1. Share your personal theologies of work (question 1, p. 17). Discuss your similarities and differences with each other.
2. What present-day values did you infer from the law of gleaning? Discuss similarities and differences.
3. What present-day values did you infer from the law of limited cropping? Discuss.
4. What present-day values did you infer from the law of the first fruits? Discuss.
5. What present-day values did you infer from the law of interest-free loans? Discuss.
6. What present-day values did you infer from the law of tithing? Discuss.
7. Now turn to the five primary work values you listed on page 20. Have each person share his or her list. Ask each other for further clarification, expanded responses and so on. But do not judge. We are here to help each other get to know ourselves better, not to criticize, commend or offer advice.

   After discussion, record your top three work values, in order of priority and in your own words.

First _____

Second _____

Third _____

Looking Ahead
Before your next meeting, record on page 51 the conclusions from pages 18-20 and 20-21; then complete the exercises on pages 22-24.

Notes
[4]It may be helpful in completing this section to consult chapter three of J. V. Taylor, *Enough Is Enough: A Biblical Call for Moderation in a Consumer-Oriented Society* (Minneapolis: Augsburg Publishing House, 1975).
[5]From U.S. Department of Labor, *Dictionary of Occupational Titles*, vol. II, 3rd ed. (Washington, D.C.: Government Printing Office, 1965), p. 654.
[6]Ibid.

PART II/ABILITIES
UNIT 4/*Life Abilities*

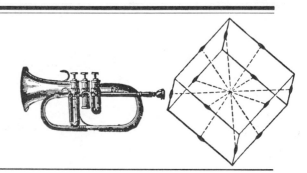

□ INDIVIDUAL EXERCISE

"And he has filled him with the Spirit of God, with ability, with intelligence, with knowledge, and with all craftsmanship, to devise artistic designs" (Ex. 35:31-32). Such were the credentials of Bezalel, Moses' chief artisan in wood, metal and stone who was given the task of making the wilderness sanctuary because his areas of expertise were recognized.

Knowing your abilities is important in evaluating career options. Bezalel's profile of skills includes life abilities (wisdom, understanding and knowledge) as well as work abilities (wood, metal and stone working). Part two will help you clarify your own life and work abilities.

Group members can serve each other by identifying abilities in each other. We live so close to our strengths that we are frequently unaware of them. We tend to think, "Anybody can do that." Through sensitive interaction you can help each other realistically break that barrier.

1. On the chart below, list under "Small Successes," ten to fifteen small successes that you have experienced within the past ten years. (For example: ran in a marathon; started a Bible study; made a Christmas gift.) Do not be concerned about the importance·of the event or the recognition you received, just whether it meant something to you.

A O	G H	$	S	10	Small Successes	Abilities
A O	G H	$	S	10		
A O	G H	$	S	10		
A O	G H	$	S	10		
A O	G H	$	S	10		
A O	G H	$	S	10		
A O	G H	$	S	10		
A O	G H	$	S	10		
A O	G H	$	S	10		
A O	G H	$	S	10		
A O	G H	$	S	10		
A O	G H	$	S	10		
A O	G H	$	S	10		
A O	G H	$	S	10		
A O	G H	$	S	10		
A O	G H	$	S	10		

Next, for each success listed, circle either *A* (if you accomplished it alone) or *O* (if you accomplished it with others); circle either *G* (if the success was goal oriented) or *H* (if it just happened); circle *$* if the success cost $5 or more; circle *S* if the success was seasonal; finally, circle *10* if you hope this success will be part of your life ten years from now. Do not fill in the "Abilities" column until your next group meeting.

2. There are many abilities that are a part of one's overall way of life and that are transferable (that is, we use them in many different settings). They are called adaptive skills. As they are used to fit into new settings, one grows as a person and the skills mature.

For Christians there is a direct relationship between growing spiritually and developing adaptive skills. The apostle Peter was excited about the privilege of participating in the divine nature and the biblical promises that promote that growth. Below you will (1) study the seven qualities Peter used to define this everexpanding spiritual development and (2) consider how these "growth edges" may be expressed through one's adaptive skills. Finally, (3) in your group, you will help each other identify and verify your personal adaptive skills.

Read 2 Peter 1:3-11. Peter states that the promises given by the Holy Spirit through the apostles can be used to promote spiritual growth. He also indicates in verse 8 that we can possess these qualities in increasing measure. The chart gives other Scripture passages to help you familiarize yourself with these qualities and discover your growth opportunities.

Biblical Growth Edges Seven qualities from 2 Pet. 1:3-11 that one may develop.	**Biblical Promises** Consider each of the Bible references below. Decide how they may be useful in promoting the spiritual growth Peter recommends. Add other promises you may know about.
1. *Virtue/Goodness* —firmly committed to practicing right behavior; doing good	*1 Corinthians 10:6-13 (especially v. 13).* How can this promise help promote virtue?
2. *Knowledge/Understanding* —learning from experience	*Colossians 2:1-8 (especially vv. 2-3).* How does the love that unites believers in Christ increase one's knowledge?
3. *Self-control/Temperance* —being responsible for one's behavior	*Romans 6:11-14 (especially v. 14).* What effect would claiming this promise have on one's self-control?
4. *Steadfastness/Patience* —showing endurance	*John 14:16-21 (especially vv. 16 and 18).* Why can Christians practice patience?
5. *Godliness/Reverence* —worshiping God	*Philippians 3:1-4 (especially vv. 1 and 3).* What attitudes do and do not underlie worshipfulness?
6. *Brotherly Affection/Kindness* —being fair; giving others a chance	*Colossians 3:12-14 (especially vv. 12-13).* How should being "God's chosen ones" influence our relationships?
7. *Love/Charity* —caring about others; agreeing with God that they are very valuable	*1 Peter 1:22-25 (especially v. 22).* What gives Christians the ability to love?

3. The next chart lists *adaptive skills* at the left and Peter's *growth edges* above the columns. As persons grow by adding these spiritual graces to their faith, which of the adaptive skills will they be likely to develop as a result? An *X* is placed where we see a relationship between adaptive skills and growth edges. Study these relationships to see if you agree. For example: Ask, "If I practice *virtue/goodness,* will that increase the chances that I will be *conscientious?"* If you agree, leave the *X,* but if not, circle the *X;* then proceed to "dresses appropriately." Add an *X* if you see a relationship. Then continue down the column. Proceed in the same way with the other six growth edges.

Next, in preparation for giving positive feedback to group members, designate one column for each member of the group and, although you may still be getting acquainted, check one to five of the adaptive skills you think you have observed in them. Do not fill in "How the Group Affirms Me" until your next group meeting.

Adaptive Skills — The person...	Virtue/Goodness	Knowledge/Understanding	Self-control/Temperance	Steadfastness/Patience	Godliness/Reverence	Brotherly Affection/Kindness	Love/Charity	How I Affirm Group Members	How the Group Affirms Me
is conscientious.	X		X		X		X		
dresses appropriately.			X				X		
enjoys keeping busy.			X	X					
is friendly.				X		X	X		
relates honestly.	X		X		X	X	X		
is objective, sees both sides.		X		X	X	X	X		
is open to change.	X	X			X		X		
is purposeful, goal directed.	X		X	X	X		X		
is resourceful, a creative problem solver.		X			X		X		
respects authority.	X		X	X	X		X		
is responsible.		X	X	X	X		X		
accepts self.			X		X	X	X		
is disciplined.	X		X	X	X		X		
shows empathy.				X	X	X	X		
leads wisely.		X			X	X	X		

□ GROUP DISCUSSION

Purposes
□ To identify some of each person's abilities.
□ To relate each group member's spiritual development to the development of his or her life abilities.

Discussion
1. Before starting, facilitator and group members, reread the definitions on page 8.
2. Let each person in turn share his or her list of small successes from question 1 on page 22. Group members should interact with the lists, asking clarifying questions and attributing abilities seen as inherent in some of the successes. Listen especially for verbs—all the things each person had to *do* to make it a success. As the group extracts abilities from each person's list, he or she can then record in the right-hand column those that make the most sense.
3. After your abilities column has been filled in, record below the four abilities listed which seem to be most central in your life.

1. _____
2. _____
3. _____
4. _____

4. Consider the "Biblical Growth Edges" on page 23. Share your responses to each and any additional passages you think apply.
5. Turn to the chart on page 24. Share how you related the adaptive skills to the growth edges. Then let everyone in the group share how they affirmed one group member. Mention what it was about this person that suggested certain skills to you. Consider each member in turn. Be sure to record in the right-hand column the group's affirmations of you.
6. After considering the feedback from question 3, select from the list of adaptive skills the four you most want to use in your career.

1. _____
2. _____
3. _____
4. _____

Looking Ahead
Before your next meeting, record on page 51 the conclusions on this page; then complete the individual exercise on pages 26-27.

PART II/ABILITIES
UNIT 5/*Work Abilities*

☐ INDIVIDUAL EXERCISE

1. In addition to interpersonal skills for getting along with others on the job (adaptive skills), there are also skills that are needed to get the job done. These are called performance skills. Think about some things you do well, utilizing the broadest possible range of your experience. List below five talents or skills that you either have or have experimented with.

1. _____
2. _____
3. _____
4. _____
5. _____

2. Now rate yourself on the skill categories listed below.[7]

Performance Skills

"Compared to other persons having this ability, I am probably..."	Highly Skilled	Above Average	Average	Below Average	Least Skilled	...?
(G) Intelligence: General learning ability. The ability to "catch on" or understand instructions and underlying principles. Ability to reason and make judgments. Closely related to doing well in school.						
(V) Verbal: Ability to understand meanings of words and ideas associated with them, and to use them effectively. To comprehend language, to understand relationships between words and to understand meanings of whole sentences and paragraphs. To present information or ideas clearly.						
(N) Numerical: Ability to perform arithmetic operations quickly and accurately.						
(S) Spatial: Ability to comprehend forms in space and understand relationships of plane and solid objects. May be used in such tasks as blueprint reading and in solving geometry problems. Frequently described as the ability to "visualize" objects of two or three dimensions, or to think visually of geometric forms.						
(P) Form Perception: Ability to perceive pertinent detail in objects or in pictorial or graphic material. To make visual comparisons and discriminations and see slight differences in shapes and shadings of figures and widths and lengths of lines.						

(Q) Clerical Perception: Ability to perceive pertinent detail in verbal or tabular material. To observe differences in copy, to proofread words and numbers, and to avoid perceptual errors in arithmetic computation.						
(K) Motor Coordination: Ability to coordinate eyes and hands or fingers rapidly and accurately in making precise movements with speed. Ability to make a movement response accurately and quickly.						
(F) Finger Dexterity: Ability to move the fingers and manipulate small objects with the fingers rapidly or accurately.						
(M) Manual Dexterity: Ability to move the hands easily and skillfully. To work with the hands in placing and turning motions.						
(E) Eye-Hand-Foot Coordination: Ability to move the hand and foot coordinately with each other in accordance with visual stimuli.						
(C) Color Discrimination: Ability to perceive or recognize similarities or differences in colors, or in shades or other values of the same color; to identify a particular color, or to recognize harmonious or contrasting color combinations, or to match colors accurately.						

3. Based on your answers to questions 1 and 2, (a) choose your four top performance skills; (b) comment on how you learned each skill, that is, in what situations you have used them or some aspect of them; and (c) name the people in your life who encouraged your development of each skill.

a. Four top performance skills (in any order)

b. How you learned each

c. The people who encourage you in each

_____ _____ _____

_____ _____ _____

_____ _____ _____

_____ _____ _____

□ GROUP DISCUSSION

Purpose
□ To identify some of each group member's work abilities.

Discussion
1. Consider question 3 above, and share your four top performance skills, how you learned them and the people in your life you associate with their development.

  As each group member does this, the rest can share their reactions. Offer new perspectives on how these comments fit in with previous information about the person and mention how the skills might be applied in different careers.

2. Now rank order your four skills listed in 3a of the individual exercise.

First _____

Second _____

Third _____

Fourth _____

Looking Ahead
Before your next meeting, list on page 52 the results from pages 26-27 and 28; then complete the individual exercise on page 29.

Note
[7]Ibid., p. 653.

PART III/GIFTS
UNIT 6/*Spiritual Gifts*

☐ INDIVIDUAL EXERCISE

As a Christian, your assessment of your abilities is not complete without an awareness of your spiritual gift or gifts. For the purpose of life planning, it is most useful to define a spiritual gift simply as what one does well that edifies others. You might ask, what's the difference between gifts and abilities, then?

For the Christian, the *source* is the same: both gifts (which the non-Christian does not have) and abilities are God-given. The difference is in the *effect*. A gift is always used for the common good of others, not simply for self-betterment. And the good that it does is helping others' involvement in furthering the kingdom of God. The distinction becomes even less clear, of course, when one's God-given ability is used as a gift for the edification of others.

Another distinction needs to be made: gift as an exercise rather than a possession.

Spiritual gifts have... become overly individualized. They are commonly called abilities, talents, endowments or capacities—terms which convey the idea of personal possessions or characteristics. Too often spiritual gifts are considered a matter of one's individual relationship with God. Yet Paul explains... it is not given to *have* but to *use*. The gift is not a *possession* but an *exercise* by the power of the Spirit. [Also], its purpose is the "common good."... The context is corporate, not private. Therefore, the believer does not struggle to discover his or her individual gift and then wonder where to use it. Instead, the Christian participates in the body and, sensitive to the needs of others, trusts the sovereign Spirit to manifest whatever gifts will meet the needs of the community.[8]

I don't have a *gift*, the *gift* has *me!* Or more accurately, the Holy Spirit has me to use for his own good purpose in meeting the needs of a particular body of believers. Consequently, our emphasis in this section, which is consistent with our life-planning approach in general, will be on helping you become sensitive to being a part of helping situations rather than being a gifted person as such. In short, our emphasis is more on the process than on the product.

1. Read the following biblical statements and write in your own words what they say about gifts:

Exodus 35:30-35

1 Corinthians 12:4-6, 11

1 Corinthians 12:8-10, 28; 13:1-3, 8; 14:6, 26

Romans 12:3-8

Ephesians 4:7-11

1 Peter 4:9-11

1 Corinthians 12:7; Ephesians 4:12

□ GROUP DISCUSSION

Purposes
□ To discriminate between abilities and gifts.
□ To identify the spiritual gifts listed in the biblical text.
□ To identify the source and effect of spiritual gifts.

Discussion
1. Look at page 29. In your own words, what is the difference between abilities and gifts?
What does it mean to enable others or do something for their common good?
How could a God-given ability be used as a gift? Give an example.
2. Contrast, in your own words, the difference between being in a helping situation and being a gifted person.
3. Notice that the first spiritual gifts in the Bible (Ex. 35:30-35) are practical and creative abilities, including the ability to teach craftsmanship. What does that say to you about the range of possibilities of spiritual gifts?
4. According to 1 Corinthians 12:4-6 and 11, who distributes spiritual gifts among believers?
5. What spiritual gifts did you identify from the biblical references given in the individual exercise? (Write down all the ones you found.)

6. According to 1 Corinthians 12:7, is a spiritual gift for personal possession or for community action?
7. Discuss how the following statements support the view of gifts as process rather than product.

Example A
"It's so exciting to be a part of that prayer group. We are continually seeing God answer prayer. We just share needs and concerns and by the next time we meet—Wow! One has gotten a job, another was able to witness to a friend, some other person's making an unexpectedly rapid recovery from surgery. There's so much love and joy in the group—so much to praise God for."

Example B
"Prayer meeting is boring. There ought to be people with gifts there. Someone ought to have a gift of knowledge, another a gift of helps, another faith, and so forth. I think someone should be able to pray for those who are sick and see them healed. We ought to know who we can turn to for these manifestations."

Looking Ahead
Before your next meeting, complete the individual exercise on page 31.

Note
[8]Charles E. Hummel, *Fire in the Fireplace: Contemporary Charismatic Renewal* (Downers Grove: InterVarsity Press, 1978), pp. 170-71.

PART III/GIFTS
UNIT 7/*Exercising Spiritual Gifts*

☐ INDIVIDUAL EXERCISE

Remembering that in the context of life planning a spiritual gift is anything one does that edifies others, we can move beyond the examples the Bible gives of spiritual gifts. Let's consider how we can recognize the activity of the Spirit in calling forth gifts in a group of believers. How do we do this? How do we become aware of our usefulness in helping others further the kingdom? How do we encourage others to be of use to a group of believers?

We want to help direct your attention away from your own spiritual status and toward the working of the Spirit and the communion of saints. We want you to be able to assess your role in the body. We want you to be open to the continuous working of the Holy Spirit as you move from one group of believers to another. One does not just pack up a "gift bag" with gifts to give to the next group solely based on how you were used in a previous group. The Holy Spirit can call forth different gifts from one person in different groups because each group has different needs.

1. List your ideas about how a person identifies a spiritual gift.

2. Think for a moment about your group. From what you know about each member thus far, including yourself, what are some of the ways in which you have been helpful to one another?

3. Think about the future. How can you be open to the continuous working of the Holy Spirit when you are in the company of believers, particularly when you move from one group to another?

☐ GROUP DISCUSSION

Purposes
☐ To learn to be open to the continuous leading of the Holy Spirit.
☐ To learn a procedure for the periodic assessment of the leading of the Holy Spirit.
☐ To learn how the Holy Spirit has likely been using each group member for the common good during the group discussions.

Discussion

1. Refer to question 1 in the individual exercise and share your approach to identifying spiritual gifts. What do you think about the idea that it is not possible to truly know your spiritual gift(s) outside the fellowship of believers?

2. Share your thoughts from question 2 (p. 31). Note: This discussion will lay the groundwork for the group exercise below.

3. With reference to question 3, have you been given a gift in one group of believers and then moved to a different group of believers and been given a different gift? Or was it the same gift?

How did you make the transition to a new setting with the same gift, or to a new setting and a new gift?

How did you identify your gift in the new group? How could you have identified your function in the group better?

4. To give you some practice in periodic assessment of the leading of the Holy Spirit, and to give you an opportunity to learn how you are potentially being gifted in this group, try the following exercise. Remember that you are learning a way of going about identifying your gift(s) within the larger Christian community; you are not necessarily identifying your gift(s) itself (themselves). This is a small-group exercise you can use with a group of believers anyplace, any time. Allow each person time to respond verbally to each question below before moving on to the next question. Use the first set of boxes for your own responses. Use the other sets for recording the responses from the other group members. The accumulation of this information will be important for answering question 6, which will reveal how God is using you to help others in your group.

a. Using the analogy of a body, what part of the body do you feel you function best as: a hand (sharing); an ear (listening); a tongue (talking) or another? Record the part of the body each person chooses in his or her "Ability" box.

b. What part of the body do you need at this moment from others to release you to be the person you feel God wants you to be (to express a possible gift you have been afraid or unwilling to develop): a hand, a heart or another?

What can the group do to support you? Take time, if appropriate, to respond as a group to each other's needs. Record the responses under "Need."

c. If you had the support of a Christian community that would support you completely, what activity would you like to give yourself to? Feel free to say what you think, regardless of how foolish or trivial it may seem (the group will not laugh or criticize you). Record the responses under "Wish."

d. Each one in the group should in turn face the others in the group and complete the statements, "One thing I really like about you is . . ." and "One way God has used you to help me in this group is. . . ." Under "Affirmation" record all the responses directed to each individual by the others in the group.

Name	Need	Affirmation
Ability	Wish	
Name	Need	Affirmation
Ability	Wish	
Name	Need	Affirmation
Ability	Wish	
Name	Need	Affirmation
Ability	Wish	
Name	Need	Affirmation
Ability	Wish	

5. Review the responses to the affirmations you received and ask for further clarification: "What did you mean by . . . ?" "You pointed out . . . about me, which really excites me! Could you expand it a little?"

6. As you consider the affirmations you received, list what seem to be some of your potential gifts.

1. _____

2. _____

3. _____

Looking Ahead

Before your next meeting, record on page 52 your potential gifts listed above; then complete the individual exercise on pages 35-39.

PART IV/INTERESTS
UNIT 8/*Interest Inventory*

☐ INDIVIDUAL EXERCISE

This unit will be more individual than group centered. The main input will come from the results of the Strong-Campbell Interest Inventory (SCII) or the alternate materials we have provided.

Interests are usually what people think of first when making career-related decisions. "What are your interests?" we ask others who are thinking about getting a job. *Interests are either spontaneous or enduring likes or dislikes for certain activities that are thought about or actually encountered.*

1. Interests are commonly expressed in Scripture. Considering the above definition, read the following examples and check which component(s) of the definition seem(s) to be present in each. As an illustration, the first example below has been completed. As Abraham encountered God's announcement of the impending judgment of Sodom, he spontaneously expressed dislike for the idea of righteous persons suffering along with the wicked.

	Sponta-neous	Endur-ing	Likes	Dislikes	Thought About	Actually Encoun-tered
Abraham Gen. 18:20-33	✓			✓		✓
Jacob Gen. 29:15-30						
Moses Ex. 4:1-13						
Ruth Ruth 1:8-18						
Mary Lk. 10:38-42						
Simon Acts 8:14-24						
Paul Rom. 9:1-5						

2. You will now need your results of the SCII you completed earlier. If possible, go over your inventory profile with a counselor. If you do not have results from the SCII, turn to page 38.

a. First inspect the *General Occupational Themes* box at the top of the sheet. Circle the letter of the theme(s) that is (are) average or higher according to the interpretive statement in the "results" column: **R   I   A   S   E   C**

b. Next inspect the *Basic Interest Scales* for the highest group(s) of interests and relate your findings back to the matching General Occupational Themes. (Each letter—*R*, *I*, *A* and so on— retains its own color wherever it appears on the sheet provided by the NCS/Interpretive Scoring Service.) What you want to discover is your strongest occupational theme(s) as supported by the appropriate basic interest(s).

c. You may want to inspect the related *Occupational Scales* for your strongest theme(s) to further clarify the strength of your findings. Look for consistency across all three: General Occupational Themes, Basic Interest Scales, Occupational Scales.

d. A note of encouragement: if your strongest theme is only moderately high to average or lower, this probably means there are variables other than interests (for example, values and abilities) that are more important for you in your career-decision process. In any case, circle your strongest overall occupational theme(s):

Realistic   **I**nvestigative   **A**rtistic   **S**ocial   **E**nterprising   **C**onventional

3. Now refer your conclusion to the following Occupational Orientation Reference Chart. The occupational themes on your inventory profile are listed in the left-hand column. Notice the other three sections of the chart: basic *Interest* categories (columns 2 and 3); individual and relational *Personality* characteristics (columns 4, Intrapersonal, and 5, Interpersonal); work *Environment* conditions (columns 6, Activity, and 7, Climate). Moving from left to right, read the entire entry for the General Occupational Theme(s) you circled in question 2d. You will notice that perhaps some of the words do not really seem to apply to you. This is probably because your highest theme(s) was(were) not consistently high across all three areas of the SCII (General Occupational Themes, Basic Interest Scales, Occupational Scales) and therefore not predictive of everything involved in that(those) theme(s).

Occupational Orientation Reference Chart

Theme	Interest		Personality		Environment	
			Intrapersonal	Interpersonal	Activity	Climate
Realistic	technical trade	technical supervision	practical *persistent*	*aggressive*	thing-oriented *physical*	*concrete*
Investigative	biological science	physical science	intellectual *analytical*	*reserved*	idea-oriented *thought-full*	*scholarly*
Artistic	cultural-aesthetic	verbal-linguistic	individualistic *impulsive*	*independent*	expressive *creative*	*free*
Social	social service		idealistic *religious*	*humanistic*	people-oriented *educational*	*interpersonal*
Enterprising	business contact	business executive	energetic *confident*	*dominating*	organizational *leadership*	*power-full*
Conventional	business detail		conscientious *efficient*	*conforming*	ordered *systematic*	*structured*

4. In the following Personal Occupational Orientation Chart, write in those words from the Reference Chart in question 3 that you feel particularly apply to you. Most, if not all, should be from the entry for your highest theme(s).

Personal Occupational Orientation Chart

Theme	Interest		Personality	Environment
			Intrapersonal Interpersonal	Activity Climate

5. While reviewing your results of the SCII, you perhaps noticed a basic interest that was high and a related occupation that was low. This usually happens when a person has a particular interest but does not match the style of life (the personality-characteristics and environmental-conditions columns of the occupational orientation charts) of those already successfully employed in a related occupation. Such interests can be meaningfully expressed through *avocations* or hobbies—they are something you simply enjoy. You do not have to make a living in those ways. Look at your Personal Occupational Chart above. Which of the words listed there might you consider to be primarily avocationally related? List them, if any, below. If you have gone over the SCII with a counselor, also list any of the highest of the 23 specific items from the Basic Interests Scales you consider to be noncareer oriented.

Avocational Interests

Personal Occupational Orientation	Basic Interests (Optional)
1. _____	1. _____
2. _____	2. _____
3. _____	3. _____
4. _____	4. _____

6. Now list the remaining words from the above chart which indicate your career-oriented interests. Again, if you have gone over the SCII with a counselor, also list from the remaining career-oriented items from the Basic Interests Scales those which particularly apply to you.

Career Interests

Personal Occupational Orientation	Basic Interests (Optional)

1. _____   1. _____

2. _____   2. _____

3. _____   3. _____

4. _____   4. _____

5. _____   5. _____

6. _____   6. _____

Alternative Material for Those without Results from the Strong-Campbell Interest Inventory

7. Imagine that you are attending a workshop on lifestyles.[9] When you enter, you see there are six meeting rooms, and you are asked to go first to the one that most interests you, second to the one that next most interests you, and third to any of the remaining four. To help you choose, you are given the following descriptions:

Workshop R. The people in this group will be discussing building, planting and engaging in other technical activities. They are very practical people (persistent and somewhat aggressive) and like to express themselves physically and work with things.

Workshop I. The people here will discuss working in a scientific setting. They are quite intellectual (very analytical and somewhat reserved) and like more scholarly activities centered on sharing ideas.

Workshop A. People here will discuss painting, listening to music and engaging in other aesthetic activities. They are rather individualistic (impulsive and independent) and like creative, expressive pursuits.

Workshop S. The people here will discuss helping others through various social service activities. They are somewhat idealistic (in the religious or humanistic sense) and like to work in an educational setting and be around people.

Workshop E. The people in this workshop will discuss selling, managing and doing other business-related things. The emphasis is on contact with people. They are energetic (confident and dominating) and like to function in a leadership capacity within an organizational structure.

Workshop C. The people here will discuss doing office work. The emphasis of this kind of business activity is on detail. They are very conscientious (efficient and conforming) and like a structured, highly ordered environment.

Indicate which workshops you would like to attend in order of preference.

First _____

Second _____

Third _____

8. Now go back to the descriptions of the two or three workshops you just picked and list the words that seem to particularly apply to the kind of job you would like to have.

1. _____   4. _____

2. _____   5. _____

3. _____   6. _____

□ GROUP DISCUSSION

Purpose
□ To identify the career-related interests of each group member.

Discussion
1. Turn back to page 35 and share how your brief study of the seven Bible characters deepened your understanding of the nature of interests.

2. On page 36 you interpreted your results of the SCII. (If you do not have results from the SCII, skip to question 5 below.) Review with each other how you arrived at your conclusion for question 2d. After you have cleared up any difficulties you may have had when you went over your results alone and made any necessary corrections in the occupational theme(s) you circled, record your revised version below, choosing three if possible.

General Occupational Themes

Realistic   Investigative   Artistic   Social   Enterprising   Conventional

3. Now rank these in order.

First _____   Second _____   Third _____

4. Look at pages 37-38. Share briefly your lists of avocational and career interests. Discuss each member's lists to see if any of the avocational interests might better be listed under career interests or vice versa. Record below your original or revised version of your "Career Interests" (question 6). Then skip questions 5-8 below and go to "Looking Ahead" on page 40.

Career Interests

Personal Occupational Orientation	Basic Interests (Optional)
1. _____	1. _____
2. _____	2. _____
3. _____	3. _____
4. _____	4. _____
5. _____	5. _____
6. _____	6. _____

5. If you do not have results from the SCII and therefore have not completed questions 2 through 4 above, share your conclusions from questions 7 and 8 on pages 38-39. Discuss the workshops and what you thought each would be like.

6. After talking it over in the group, record your original or revised answer from question 7, choosing at least three.

General Occupational Themes

| Realistic | Investigative | Artistic | Social | Enterprising | Conventional |

7. Now rank these in order.

First _____   Second _____   Third _____

8. Also record your original or revised conclusion from question 8.

Career Interests
Personal Occupational Orientation

1. _____

2. _____

3. _____

4. _____

5. _____

6. _____

Looking Ahead
Before your next meeting, list on page 52 the items highlighted by heavy rules from either page 39 or this page; then complete the individual exercise on pages 41-43.

Note
[9]Adapted from R. N. Bolles, *The Quick Job-Hunting Map* (Berkeley, Calif., National Career Development Project, Ten Speed Press, 1975), p. 4.

PART V/DECISION MAKING
UNIT 9/*Risk Taking and Assertiveness*

☐ INDIVIDUAL EXERCISE

While life planning requires us to know ourselves, unless we put that information to use, it is like preparing a meal that no one eats. Making decisions is the channel for completing the process. That sounds simple, but it is not. Decision making is a complex process consisting of, among other things, risk taking and assertiveness, all within the framework of God's will.

We will return to these three components: God's will, assertiveness and risk taking. However, there is one important principle that one must be aware of in making decisions. That is the distinction between the decision itself and the outcome of the decision. A good decision is made because, at the time of the decision, as much relevant information as possible is taken into account. That does not necessarily say anything about the outcome of the decision, which cannot be completely controlled. An example would be an employer firing someone without due process and then using the person's recovery and future success as verification of the wisdom of the original decision. "See, even though the decision may not have been handled as well as it could have been, and as much as that hurt you, you've turned out just fine. So the decision to let you go was for your own good." Rather, the way a decision is made is its own verification, and we most likely have in this case an example of God working in spite of—not because of—the original decision. "In other words, the 'goodness' of a decision is based on how it is made, not on how it turns out."[10]

1. Test yourself. Imagine you are arriving at a classroom, primed to take a final exam. Upon entering, students are asked to sit in alternate seats, and you choose yours near where you usually sit in the class. When the instructor hands out the exams, she mentions there are two forms of the exam, which will be distributed alternately. You take the test and leave. In talking later with a classmate, you discover the form you took was much harder than the other form. When the grades come back, your score is lower than your friend's who studied less! Was your choice of where to sit a poor decision? Why or why not?

2. Now read the following Bible passages and state in your own words what they have to say about making decisions.
Genesis 22:1-19

Galatians 3:6-9

3. Many Christians would argue that risk is at the heart of the experience of faith. Taking risks is certainly at the heart of making decisions. Note what Abraham risked in Genesis 22:1-2.

4. Uncertainty is deeply embedded in the human condition, uncertainty in spite of which choices must be made—religious choices, educational choices, career choices and so on. If our predictions were 100% certain, our deciding would be 100% easier! Read through the parable of the talents (Mt. 25:14-30) and note the risks involved.

5. How we present ourselves has important implications for life planning—not only in looking for a job but also in continuing in a job. Behavior that accurately represents our fundamental values, abilities, gifts, basic interests and knowledge of God's will for our lives is called *assertive behavior*. Behavior that represents these aspects only partially or belatedly is called *nonassertive behavior*. Behavior that manipulates, takes advantage of or violates the rights of others in those areas is called *aggressive behavior*.

Assertive behavior is important in looking for a job because it is self-enhancing, allowing you to present yourself in the best, most accurate light. Nonassertive behavior, however, will present you inaccurately and in a self-defeating way. Aggressive behavior, while self-enhancing, will be so at the expense of others. Nonassertive behavior allows others to choose your job for you; aggressive behavior chooses jobs for others; assertive behavior chooses your own job based on your needs and the needs of others. [11]

Assertive behavior is also important in continuing in a job. Most employees feel pressure to hold back their questions and criticisms relating to the organization. Employers who make decisions in secret, seemingly unconcerned with the effects on the morale of their employees, make matters even worse. They see themselves as above needing the input of employees, whom they feel they must manage rather than seek out as mutual resources. But by your being assertive, rather than nonassertive (or aggressive), you, your employer and the organization will all be helped.

6. Evaluate each of the references listed below, in its context, and determine whether the behavior that is described is assertive, nonassertive or aggressive.

Matthew 5:37 _____

Matthew 5:38-41 _____

Luke 17:3-4 _____

Romans 14:19-21 _____

Galatians 2:11-14 _____

7. Now read through the following examples and record your impressions.

Example A

Female secretary (nonthreatening posture, good eye contact and firm tone of voice): "I really do need my lunch hours to myself, to relax and get away from the pressures of the office so that I can do a better job in the afternoons. Taking your lunch order and running downtown to pick it up just does not give me the break I need and that I believe I am entitled to."

Male employer (lackadaisical posture, poor eye contact and wavering tone of voice): "You're cute when you're mad."

Example B

A person has just reviewed a report a peer has written and submitted for evaluation. Realizing how important it is that the information contained in the report be correct, feedback must be given. Which of the following would be the most useful response and why?

a.   "You know, this is really bad. Look at these errors. This is a terrible report!"
b.   "Uh, thanks. Glad you got it done. It looks pretty good."
c.   "This is a good report, particularly the suggestions you have made. I'm wondering if these two statements are quite right, though. Could you please check them over?"

8. How would you rate *your* use of the three behaviors associated with assertiveness?

Response	Never	Occasionally	Frequently	Usually
Assertive	_____	_____	_____	_____
Nonassertive	_____	_____	_____	_____
Aggressive	_____	_____	_____	_____

□ GROUP DISCUSSION

Purposes
□ To understand how a good decision is made.
□ To identify each group member's approach to risk taking.
□ To identify each group member's level of assertiveness.

Discussion

1. Turn back to the classroom situation described on page 41. Discuss how each of you responded.

2. On page 41 (question 2), you read about God testing Abraham. What really mattered to Abraham—the decision he had to make or the outcome? What was Abraham's priority as a decision maker?

3. On page 41 (question 3), you recorded your thoughts about the risk Abraham took in exercising faith. What did Abraham risk?

Who was the object of his faith?

Do you think the amount of risk added to or subtracted from the strength of Abraham's faith? How?

4. In question 4, you noted the involvement of risk in the parable of the talents. Discuss the interaction of faith, fear and risk in the parable.

5. Let's try a group experiment. Let's say yours is a group of strangers who have been called together by an anonymous donor. You are each given $500 and the following choices:

a. Take your money and go home.

b. Pool half of your money with an equal amount from each of the other group members and invest the total amount in a mutually agreed-upon security. If your group can agree on the security, the donor will double the investment; if you cannot agree, you must give back the entire investment to the donor.

c. Decide as a group what item from a catalog you will buy with a pooled amount made up of the amount each of you feels he or she can contribute. The group must not only agree on the single item and what to do with it, but to further complicate things, if you buy now you will save 25% and be certain of receiving the item; if you buy a month from now you will save 75% but stand a 25% chance of not receiving the item, in which case your money will not be refunded.

d. Same condition as choice (c) with the added stipulation that the contributions are made anonymously.

Give each person in the group ten pieces of paper, each representing $50. Go through the four choices and decide how you would individually respond. Reveal your choice to the group, distribute the pieces of paper accordingly, and negotiate as necessary.

Having concluded the exercise, now discuss the following:

Did you risk anything? Why or why not?

Were you consistent in your approach to all four choices?

What factors entered into your willingness to risk (such as your economic situation, the fact that it was unearned money, your desire to buy something for someone in need, peer pressure, your distrust of others' sense of fair play)?

Does your behavior in this exercise fairly accurately represent your general approach to risk taking?

6. As a summary statement, write down how you should take your approach to risk taking into consideration when you make career-related decisions.

7. Review as a group your responses to question 6 on page 42. Discuss each person's reasoning and the similarities and differences among group members.

8. Review your impression of Example A (p. 43) and discuss the following:

Was the secretary being assertive, nonassertive or aggressive? Why?

Was the employer being assertive, nonassertive or aggressive? Why?

What would an assertive response have been for the employer?

9. In Example B, which would be the best response? Why?

10. Discuss with the group how you rated yourself on assertiveness (p. 43, question 8). What would you like to change? Why?

11. As a summary statement, write down how you should take your level of assertiveness into consideration when you make career-related decisions.

Share your answer with the group.

Looking Ahead

The conclusions reached in this unit will be used in future activities but you do not need to flip ahead to record them. All you need to do before your next meeting is to complete the individual exercise on pages 46-48.

Notes

[10]H. B. Gelalt, B. Varenhorst, R. Carey and G. P. Miller, *Decisions and Outcomes* (New York: College Entrance Examination Board, 1973), p. 9.

[11]See R. D. Alberti and M. L. Emmons, *Your Perfect Right: A Guide to Assertive Behavior*, 2nd ed. (San Luis Obispo: Impact, 1974), p. 11.

PART V/DECISION MAKING
UNIT 10/*God's Will*

☐ INDIVIDUAL EXERCISE

We have previously stated that the framework for risk taking and assertiveness is God's will. When referring to God's will, some Christians talk about God's best compared to God's second best. Such talk suggests that for each person God has a fixed occupation and a definite place for that work to be done. Others discuss God's will in terms of *directive will* versus *permissive will*. Again, the implication is that God has only one thing in mind for each of us, and anything less than that will merely be tolerated.

Seriously committed believers in Jesus Christ certainly want their lives to be pleasing to him. We suggest, however, that the way to express one's concern with pleasing God in the area of career choice is to emphasize God's ongoing involvement in the life-planning process.

1. The New Testament most often uses one of two words when referring to God's will. One of the words for *will (thelo)* means "desire," "preferred design" or "wish"; the other *(boulomai)* usually refers to "the imposing of a decree" or "a fixed outcome," but in certain contexts it may also mean "wish." There are two lists of Scripture verses below, one for each *will* word—*will* as desire or preference *(theo)* versus *will* as executive decree *(boulomai)*. Fill in the two charts, studying the context for each reference to decide (1) the meaning of *will* in that setting, (2) the person that *will* affects, (3) how that person is affected by it and (4) any overall observations that come out of your study.

Will as Desire (Possible meanings: desire; preferred design; wish)

Reference	Which Possible Meaning?	Who Is Doing the "Willing"?	How Is He or She Affected?	My Observations
Rom. 12:1-8 "... prove what is the *will* of God..."	design	the "living sacrifice" Christian	my transformed thought processes will identify God's design for me	suggest that God's will relates more to the quality of my life than to the function I perform.
1 Thess. 4:3-8 "... this is the *will* of God..."	design	Christians	God wants me to lead a holy life.	sanctification being set apart focuses on the quality of life again.

Reference	Which Possible Meaning?	Who Is Doing the "Willing"?	How Is He or She Affected?	My Observations
1 Cor. 12:18-26 "... God arranged ... as he *chose*..."				
Eph. 5:15-17 "... the *will* of the Lord..."				
Phil. 2:12-13 "... to *will* and to work for his good pleasure."				
1 Thess. 5:18 "... the *will* of God in Christ Jesus..."				
1 Tim. 2:1-4 "... who *desires* all..."				
1 Pet. 3:14-17 "... if that should be God's *will*..."				

Reference	Which Possible Meaning?	Who Is Doing the "Willing"?	How Is He or She Affected?	My Observations
1 Jn. 2:15-17 "... the *will* of God..."				

Will as Decree (Possible Meanings: decree; fixed outcome; wish)

Reference	Which Possible Meaning?	Who Is Doing the "Willing"?	How Is He or She Affected?	My Observations
Heb. 6:17-18 "... when God *desired* to show ... the unchangeable character of his purpose..."	*wish* / *fixed outcome*	*God* / *God*	*God willingly...* / *... bound himself to keeping his promise to Abraham.*	*God is irreversibly committed to offering us salvation.*
Acts 13:34-36 "... he had served the *counsel* of God..." (Note: compare 1 Sam. 16:6-13.)				
1 Cor. 12:4, 8-11 "... as he *wills*."				
Eph. 1:11-13 "... the *counsel* of his will..."				

□ GROUP DISCUSSION

Purposes
□ To understand the biblical meanings of the word *will*, when referring to God's will.
□ To identify how each group member's understanding of God's will affects his or her career-related decisions.

Discussion
1. Compare your observations from your study of the two uses of the word *will* (pp. 46-48). Help each other correct any misunderstandings.
2. Below are four propositions about God's will. Consider whether you agree fully, in part or totally disagree. Record your personal conclusion after the group discusses each proposition.

Propositions	Observations and Conclusions
a. God's executive decrees are usually requirements he imposes upon himself while he still allows us freedom of choice.	
b. God's preferred will has to do with the quality of one's life. He has no "permissive will" as such, but will provide the ability to fulfill his expectations. No one needs to live below the standard God expects.	
c. God's best was rejected at the Fall. Since then, all expressions of his will are in one sense a redemptive second best. At whatever point a person seeks to please God, however, God's redemptive power is activated to help him or her make the best of his or her life.	
d. At the core, God's preferred will has to do with living in fellowship with him. Within the context of this interaction with the Holy Spirit, each individual is responsible for defining specific career objectives for himself or herself.	

3. Now think through all the various aspects of God's will discussed by your group and summarize your position.

4. As a summary statement, write down your understanding of how God's will affects your career-related decisions.

Looking Ahead
Before your next meeting, complete the individual exercise on pages 50-55.

PART VI/INVESTIGATING CAREER POSSIBILITIES
UNIT 11/*Assets and Abilities*

☐ INDIVIDUAL EXERCISE

There are four parts to career planning:
☐ Knowing the assets and abilities you have or are developing.
☐ Identifying the calling(s) appropriate for you.
☐ Defining your career objective(s).
☐ Knowing how to carry out your career plan(s).

Each of these four will be considered in detail in this section. You already have much of the information you need to evaluate various careers. Keep in mind that most persons make two or three major career changes during their lives and often use the same abilities in each of these differing settings. As your education and experience produce changes and growth, the information in this section can easily be modified. If you update these items once every year, for example, you will increase your preparedness for change and opportunities for an abundant life.

By completing the previous sections you have developed an invaluable awareness as to your values, abilities, gifts, interests and decision-making style. Career satisfaction is in direct proportion to the extent people have opportunity to use their assets and abilities in achieving worthwhile goals. In the previous sections the most important items have been highlighted by heavy rules. They provide answers to such questions as: What do I do well? How do I know what I really want to do? How can I direct my growth experiences toward my long-range goals? You are now ready to draw together all these insights and ratings to use in your planning.

1. You will notice that some of the headings for the data below include the letters "DOL." These stand for **D**epartment **of L**abor and the personal characteristics marked "DOL" are used in their publications to rate jobs and careers. The significance of this will be explained in greater detail in the next unit.

The results from units 2 through 8 should be recorded below already. If so, review your findings. If not, record them now. You are then ready to go on to questions 2 and 3, beginning on page 52.

Values (p. 15, question 7)

First _____

Second _____

Third _____

Values As Suggested by Others (p. 16, question 9)

1. _____
2. _____
3. _____

DOL Temperament Code (pp. 18-20, question 3)

Each Work Value has a number following it. For each value you responded to positively, circle the number in the list below. If the same choice appears twice, add a check mark beside the circle.

I prefer work situations involving:

1. Variety of duties, changes
2. Repetition, standard procedures
3. Specific instructions
4. Planning, being in control
5. Dealing with people, team effort
6. Working alone
7. Influencing people
8. Performing under stress, taking risks
9. Sensory or judgmental criteria
0. Measurable or verifiable criteria
X. Interpretation, personal viewpoint
Y. Precise attainment of standards

DOL Work Values (pp. 20-21, question 5)

1 dealing with objects	*Pair I*	**6** communication with people
2 business activities	*Pair II*	**7** technical or scientific activities
3 routine-concrete	*Pair III*	**8** creative-abstract
4 social improvement	*Pair IV*	**9** technical advances
5 reward of prestige	*Pair V*	**0** tangible payoff

Work Values (p. 21, question 7)

First _____
Second _____
Third _____

Abilities As Suggested by Others (p. 25, question 3)

1. _____
2. _____
3. _____
4. _____

Adaptive Skills (p. 25, question 6)

1. _____
2. _____
3. _____
4. _____

DOL Aptitude Areas (pp. 26-27, question 2)

	Highly Skilled	Above Average	Average	Below Average	Least Skilled	?
(G) Intelligence						
(V) Verbal						
(N) Numerical						
(S) Spatial						
(P) Form Perception						
(Q) Clerical Perception						
(K) Motor Coordination						
(F) Finger Dexterity						
(M) Manual Dexterity						
(E) Eye-Hand-Foot Coordination						
(C) Color Discrimination						

Performance Skills (p. 28, question 2)

First _____

Second _____

Third _____

Fourth _____

Potential Spiritual Gifts (p. 34, question 6)

1. _____
2. _____
3. _____

General Occupational Themes (p. 39, question 3 or p. 40, question 7)

First _____

Second _____

Third _____

Career-oriented Interests (p. 39, question 4 or p. 40, question 8)

Personal Occupational Orientation   Basic Interests (Optional)

_____   _____

_____   _____

_____   _____

_____   _____

_____   _____

2. In the following exercise you will rate yourself in three additional areas that are used in the U.S. Department of Labor (DOL) career literature.

DOL Physical Demands[12]

Cross out part or all of any demands or levels that are unacceptable to you.

1. Lifting, carrying, pushing and/or pulling:

S—Sedentary: usually seated; maximum lifting 10 lbs.

L—Light work: some walking and standing; lifting 20 lbs.

M—Medium work: lifting 50 lbs.

H—Heavy work, active: lifting 100 lbs.

V—Very heavy work: very physical, lifting over 100 lbs.

2. Climbing, balancing.

3. Stooping, kneeling, crouching, crawling.

4. Reaching, handling, fingering, feeling.

5. Talking, hearing.

6. Seeing: judging shape, size, distance, motion, color.

DOL "SVP" and "GED" Levels

Look through the Specific Vocational Preparation (SVP) levels listed in the left-hand column below. Circle the highest level you are willing to consider in order to meet a career goal. "SVP" may be on-the-job or apprentice training, technical school or college work. To help you decide, the right-hand column, General Educational Development (GEV), lists the corresponding levels of formal educational achievement.

Specific Vocation Preparation[13]		General Educational Development	
Level	Time	Degree	Level
1	Short demonstration only	High School	1-3
2	Anything beyond short demonstration up to and including 30 days		
3	Over 30 days up to and including 3 months		
4	Over 3 months up to and including 6 months		
5	Over 6 months up to and including 1 year		
6	Over 1 year up to and including 2 years	1 or 2 years Technical School or College	4
7	Over 2 years up to and including 4 years	4 years College	5
8	Over 4 years up to and including 10 years	Master's Degree	6
9	Over 10 years	Doctor's Degree	

DOL Data/People/Things[14]

The *Dictionary of Occupational Titles* evaluates vocations for the skills needed and reports them as data skills, skills with people and skills with things. These are skills listed on the following pages. As you study each list, circle each level that reflects your personal skills. You may circle several numbers in each list. The more complex levels, skills requiring more education and/or experience have lower numbers (0, 1 and 2) while the least difficult have higher numbers (6, 7 and 8).

Review the summary information on pages 50-52. This will help you rate yourself in these three skill areas.

Data Skills: Abilities related to the development or use of information, knowledge and ideas. Data are creations of the mind using symbols, words and numbers.

0   *Synthesizing* is thinking deeply about groups of facts and, as a result, developing new interpretations or discovering new facts.

1   *Coordinating* is deciding the order, time or place for events based on one's examination of the facts; it is also putting these plans into action or reporting one's plans.

2   *Analyzing* is logically understanding data and determining their meaning or usefulness; it frequently is figuring out alternative actions using one's evaluation of the facts.

3   *Compiling* is collecting, classifying and reporting information; it often includes carrying out some prescribed action indicated by the information.

4   *Computing* is using arithmetic and applying the results in reports or taking specific action.

5   *Copying* is entering or posting data on forms or into a record, or transcribing data from some source such as notes or dictation.

6   *Comparing* is making judgments on readily observed functions, structures or composition of things, data or people by noting what is the same or different.

Next, complete the statements below:

The highest level of *data skills* I use and feel confident about is: _____ .

Some of the activities in which I have used these data skills are:

People Skills: Ways persons or even animals are dealt with.

0   *Mentoring* is dealing with individuals' total personality to help them solve their problems by applying one's professional knowledge of legal, scientific, counseling or spiritual principles to their needs.

1   *Negotiating* is jointly arriving at a mutually acceptable conclusion or plan with others as a result of getting people to candidly exchange information and opinions.

2   *Instructing* is applying specialized methods of explanation, demonstration or supervised practice to teach or train others (including animals) in a specific area of knowledge or behavior.

3   *Supervising* is deciding what needs to be done, when and how, and explaining the work to a group of workers, making assignments to them, encouraging high quality, productivity and harmonious interpersonal relationships.

4   *Diverting* is providing entertainment for others, to be amusing.

5   *Persuading* is influencing others in favor of a product, service or point of view.

6   *Speaking-Signaling* is sending or exchanging information with others by talking or using some system of signs, including giving directions.

7   *Serving* is giving attention to the needs or requests of people or animals, or the expressed or obvious wishes of people. It involves immediate response.

8   *Taking Instruction-Helping* is being able to take orders; it applies to "nonlearning" helpers.

Next, complete the following statements:

The highest level of *people skills* I use and feel confident about is: _____ .

Some of the activities in which I have used these are:

Thing Skills: The ways in which workers use or interact with nonliving equipment and tangible materials.

0   *Setting up* is assembling complicated machines or equipment; adjusting tools, jigs, fixtures and attachments so that they will operate properly.

1   *Precision Working* is using one's body along with equipment of some kind to precisely change the form of objects or materials. To meet these exact standards requires considerable judgment in selecting the materials and the appropriate tools and in adjusting or using the tools.

2   *Operating-Controlling* involves starting, stopping, checking and adjusting the progress of machines or equipment. Operating machines includes setting up and adjusting the machine and materials as the work progresses. Controlling relates to checking and regulating such things as temperature, pressure, speed and flow by means of dials, valves and other devices.

3   *Driving-Operating* requires controlling and steering power equipment that must be guided in order to move people or materials. It involves such activities as observing dials, estimating distances, determining speed and direction, turning cranks or wheels and pushing or pulling levers to operate such things as cranes, conveyor systems, tractors and hoists.

4   *Manipulating* means using body members or special devices to work, move, guide, or place objects or materials. It involves some rather easily attained precision in selecting appropriate tools, objects or materials.

5   *Tending* is starting, stopping and observing the functioning of machines and equipment. It involves adjusting materials or controls of the machine by means of valves, guides and switches. Little judgment is involved in making these adjustments.

6   *Feeding-Offbearing* is putting materials in or removing them from machines that are automatic or operated by others.

7   *Handling* involves moving or carrying materials by using body members or simple hand-tools or devices. It requires little or no judgment with regard to precision or in selecting materials and tools.

Finally, complete these statements:

The highest level of *thing skills* I can confidently perform is: _____ .
Activities requiring me to use these skills include:

3. Now review the section on risk taking (p. 44, question 6), assertiveness (p. 45, question 11) and God's will (p. 49, question 3) and briefly list the principles you feel are important for you to follow in decision making.

Principles for Decision Making

□ GROUP DISCUSSION

Purposes
□ To confirm and/or modify the perceptions group members have of each other's career-related attributes.
□ To identify the factors that will most influence each group member's vocational choices.

Discussion
1. Each person share the results of the *values* as suggested by others and *abilities* as suggested by others listed on pages 50-51. Because you know each other better now than when these values and abilities were first suggested, you can confirm, add to or suggest deletions as each person shares in turn.

2. Go around the group with each person telling his or her skill levels selected for the data/people/things categories (pp. 54-55). After receiving feedback from the group, fill in the code numbers for each category that best identifies your highest level of operative skills.

DOL D/P/T Code
Data _____ People _____ Things _____

(Note: The DOL *Dictionary of Occupational Titles*, DOT, assigns unique nine-digit numbers to each of the thousands of jobs it defines. The middle three digits are the D/P/T Code; for example, the computer operator nine-digit number is 213.*362*-010; the *362* means that a person in this job needs data skills at level 3 or above, low people skills at level 6 and rather high things skills, level 2. We'll be using this more in the next unit.)

3. Finally, the members of the group can minister to you and you to them as you each assign priorities to your attributes. Let each member ask the group, "What do you see as my key attributes: those values, skills, abilities, gifts that I will most likely use in my career?" Record the group's suggestions to you below. Underline those you agree with and add to their suggestions any that you favor but the group failed to mention.

Looking Ahead
The next step is to identify representative career options that fit your profile of strengths. The information and individual exercise on pages 57-67 will help you prepare for the next meeting.

Notes
[12]Department of Labor, *Dictionary of Occupational Titles*, 3rd ed. pp. 654-55.
[13]Ibid., p. 653.
[14]From U.S. Department of Labor, *Dictionary of Occupational Titles*, 4th ed. (Washington, D.C. Government Printing Office, 1977), pp. 1369-71.

PART VI/INVESTIGATING CAREER POSSIBILITIES
UNIT 12/*Career Options*

□ INDIVIDUAL EXERCISE

1. Before answering the following questions, you may wish to review Ecclesiastes 9:10, 1 Corinthians 15:58 and Colossians 3:17. If all work is to be done using full effort, as a stand-in for Christ and with confidence in its worth, is there, for the Christian, such a thing as secular employment? Sacred employment? Why or why not?

2. Having finally completed the self-assessment phase of life planning, you are now able to consider various career options. You will want to identify as many options as possible since your unique set of characteristics can be used in several career settings. As mentioned earlier, the initial sources of career information you will use have been developed by the U.S. Department of Labor which has reported its findings in three books:

The Dictionary of Occupational Titles (DOT). Numbers, lists and defines thousands of jobs according to logical and industrial categories.

The Guide for Occupational Exploration (GOE). Groups occupations together according to the traits needed by the workers employed in those occupations. Assigns each occupation to one of sixty-six Worker Trait Groups—so each job title gains a "WTG" number in addition to its DOT number.

The Occupational Outlook Handbook (OOH). Reports on work environments, skills and education needed, probable remuneration and benefits, future demand and sources of additional information. The information is indexed using both job titles and DOT numbers.

To make your use of these publications easier we have prepared appendix A, "Bridges to Careers in General" and appendix B, "Bridges to Specific Careers." Appendix A relates your occupational themes and academic studies to the Worker Trait Group (WTG) numbers. Appendix B lists representative occupations according to WTG numbers.

Step 1. Turn to appendix A, Chart 1, pages 98-99, and look in the "Education or Training" column for academic subjects in which you have done well. Check these. Compare your three General Occupation Themes (p. 52) with the letters assigned the subjects you checked. Circle those letters that match. For example, if you have enjoyed a course in Finance and selected "E" as one of your three themes, the Finance entry in appendix A will look like this:

✓ Finance   07.01; 07.02; 07.03; 07.04;   (E)
                            07.05; 08.01; 11.02; 11.05;
                            11.06; 11.11; 11.12

Step 2. Notice the Guide for Selection of Potential Career Areas (Guide sheet) pages 119-20 at the very end of the book. Carefully remove this sheet from your book. Turn again to appendix A, Chart 1. Select three to five checked-subject/circled-theme combinations that interest you most from among those for which you have a subject and theme match, numbering these 1 to 5 in the margin. Notice the several Worker Trait Group numbers listed with each academic subject. You will also find a list of these WTG numbers on the back of your Guide sheet. On the Guide sheet, place a check after each WTG number that follows your numbered academic interests in Chart 1 (pp. 98-99).

For example, if you checked and circled Accounting and C, Finance and E, and General Clerical and C, you would have identified three subject areas that all three have the WTG #07.01 associated with them. In the WTG listing on the Guide sheet (pp. 119-20), you will then have three checks following 07.01.

Step 3. Now notice the top portion of the Guide sheet. Here you will summarize much of the personal characteristics data listed in unit 11. Find the Occupational Themes section of the Guide sheet.

Write a *1*, *2*, and *3* above the three themes you listed on page 52. If on page 52, for example, you listed Social first, Artistic second and Enterprising third, this section of the Guide sheet will look like this:

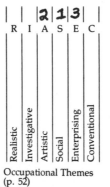

Occupational Themes
(p. 52)

Next, on page 51 find your DOL Temperament Code ratings. For each temperament that you circled or checked, put an arrow (↑) above the number on your Guide sheet. Continue to use arrows (↑) to indicate DOL Work Values and Adaptive Skills (both p. 51). Here is an example:

Next, to code the items in the DOL Aptitude Areas, turn to page 52. If you rated (G) Intelligence as Highly Skilled or Above Average, put an *H* in the box above *G* on your Guide sheet. Or, use *A* to indicate Average or *M* (Minimal) for Below Average or Least Skilled. Continue to code each aptitude using this system, as in the example below.

In the Educational Levels section, first study the Key on the Guide sheet. Refer to the DOL "SPV" and "GED" LEVELS, page 53, and in the code area above "From/To" indicate the least to the greatest educational effort you are willing to make. For example, T/G would indicate that you expect to complete a minimum of two years (T) of post-high-school training but are willing to invest as much as 10 years (G) is preparation for your career.

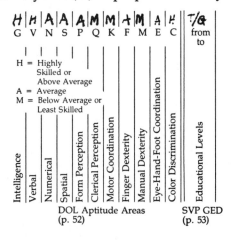

Step 4. Now you are ready to cross the second bridge in appendix A. Turn to Chart 2, pages 100-103. Follow the instructions you find on the bottom of your Guide sheet, headed "Guide for Selection of Potential Careers Areas."

Step 5. The goal of what you have done with appendix A, Chart 2, is to identify several options to consider in detail. Turn to Chart 2 and study carefully each Worker Trait Group for which you circled the various personal characteristics. Decide which groups you wish to investigate further. Your first source to use in your investigation is the *Guide for Occupational Exploration* (GOE). You should find this publication in your school's career counseling center or placement office, or at your public library. Using the Worker Trait Group number of the first career area from Chart 2 that has potential for you, look up that area in the GOE. If, for example, you have several of the related characteristics for "05.01 Engineering," and it interests you, you can turn to the "05.01" section of the GOE. Here you will find nearly two pages of specific engineering occupations listed in six subgroupings. You can read through the introductory materials and then study the list of occupations. On page 60, make a list of those occupations that you wish to consider further. Your list might look like this:

My Possible Careers

WTG#	Job	DOT#	Notes
05.01.01	laser technician	019.181-010	research; physics major, OK!
05.01.02	health physicist	079.021-010	environmental protection physics plus courses in biology needed.
05.01.05	sales-engineer electronics	003.151-014	sales will need physics plus courses in economics and marketing.

In order to make effective notes you may need to look under the DOT# in the *Dictionary of Occupational Titles* (DOT) to read a brief descriptive paragraph about each job. Continue to examine each option from Chart 2.

My Possible Careers

WTG #	Job	DOT #	Notes

(Note: As you read about these jobs in the DOT you may find other jobs in the same genre that interest you. For example, you might be studying "11.02—Librarian—100.127-014" and in that same "100." category you will find "Library Director—100.117-010" and "Aquisitions Librarian —100.267-010." These may also interest you. If so and if you need the WTG numbers for these new leads, they can be found in appendix D of the GOE.)

As you find jobs that seem especially interesting, you will want to use the third basic reference book, *The Occupational Outlook Handbook* (OOH). From it you can add to your notes the working conditions, salary range, how many new employees are needed each year and where you can obtain more information.

If the GOE and OOH are not available to you, you will find in Chart 1 of appendix B (pp. 104-11) a few job titles that are representative of the listings found in the GOE. Look in appendix B under the WTG numbers of careers for which you circled various personal characteristics in Chart 2, appendix A (pp. 100-103).

If you wish to work in the Christian setting, Chart 2 of appendix B (pp. 112-15) relates selected occupations and Christian work environments.

Step 6. Having completed your information gathering, it is time to narrow your choices by identifying careers to be evaluated in depth. Select at least three careers from among those you researched and listed on page 60, "My Possible Careers." Prepare a Career Option Evaluation Sheet for each. See example on page 62.

This person grouped together some jobs that draw on a common core of personal characteristics. Notice that Speech Pathology belongs to the same DOT genre (076.) as his or her first and second choices but has a different Worker Trait Group (WTG) number. By contrast, Dental Hygienist has the same WTG number (10.02) but belongs to a different DOT family of jobs (078.). Also, he or she could have done a separate Career Option Evaluation Sheet for each career title.

When you meet as a group you will share the information from your Career Option Evaluation Sheets and discuss the next steps. Five blank forms follow. If you need more, use blank sheets of paper.

Career Option Evaluation Sheet

1st: WTG # _____ Career Title _____ DOT # _____

Associated Career Titles and Numbers

2nd: WTG # _____ Career Title _____ DOT # _____

3rd: WTG # _____ Career Title _____ DOT # _____

4th: WTG # _____ Career Title _____ DOT # _____

1. How does this career option fit my values (see Work Values, Chart 2, pp. 100-103; and pp. 74-75)?

2. How am I qualified by abilities, skills and gifts for this option (see Temperament, Aptitude, and Skills, Chart 2)?

3. How does this option meet my career-oriented interests (see Occupational Themes, Chart 2, pp. 100-103; and note your career-oriented interests [p. 52] from your SCII results)?

4. What levels of physical demands are required (compare "DOL Physical Demands," p. 53)?

5. What additional education does this option require (compare DPT, p. 56; see Educational Levels, Chart 2, pp. 100-103)?

_____

Decision (See "Principles for Decision Making," p. 55)

_____ Acceptable   _____ Unacceptable   _____ Continue Research

Follow-through plans . . .

Career Option Evaluation Sheet

1st: WTG # _____ Career Title _____ DOT # _____

Associated Career Titles and Numbers

2nd: WTG # _____ Career Title _____ DOT # _____

3rd: WTG # _____ Career Title _____ DOT # _____

4th: WTG # _____ Career Title _____ DOT # _____

1. How does this career option fit my values (see Work Values, Chart 2, pp. 100-103; and pp. 74-75)?

2. How am I qualified by abilities, skills and gifts for this option (see Temperament, Aptitude, and Skills, Chart 2)?

3. How does this option meet my career-oriented interests (see Occupational Themes, Chart 2, pp. 100-103; and note your career-oriented interests [p. 52] from your SCII results)?

4. What levels of physical demands are required (compare "DOL Physical Demands," p. 53)?

5. What additional education does this option require (compare DPT, p. 56; see Educational Levels, Chart 2, pp. 100-103)?

Decision (See "Principles for Decision Making," p. 55)

_____ Acceptable   _____ Unacceptable   _____ Continue Research

Follow-through plans . . .

Career Option Evaluation Sheet

1st: WTG # _____ Career Title _____ DOT # _____

Associated Career Titles and Numbers

2nd: WTG # _____ Career Title _____ DOT # _____

3rd: WTG # _____ Career Title _____ DOT # _____

4th: WTG # _____ Career Title _____ DOT # _____

1. How does this career option fit my values (see Work Values, Chart 2, pp. 100-103; and pp. 74-75)?

2. How am I qualified by abilities, skills and gifts for this option (see Temperament, Aptitude, and Skills, Chart 2)?

3. How does this option meet my career-oriented interests (see Occupational Themes, Chart 2, pp. 100-103; and note your career-oriented interests [p. 52] from your SCII results)?

4. What levels of physical demands are required (compare "DOL Physical Demands," p. 53)?

5. What additional education does this option require (compare DPT, p. 56; see Educational Levels, Chart 2, pp. 100-103)?

Decision (See "Principles for Decision Making," p. 55)

_____ Acceptable   _____ Unacceptable   _____ Continue Research

Follow-through plans...

Career Option Evaluation Sheet

1st: WTG # _____ Career
Title _____ DOT # _____

Associated Career Titles and Numbers

2nd: WTG # _____ Career
Title _____ DOT # _____

3rd: WTG # _____ Career
Title _____ DOT # _____

4th: WTG # _____ Career
Title _____ DOT # _____

1. How does this career option fit my values (see Work Values, Chart 2, pp. 100-103; and pp. 74-75)?

2. How am I qualified by abilities, skills and gifts for this option (see Temperament, Aptitude, and Skills, Chart 2)?

3. How does this option meet my career-oriented interests (see Occupational Themes, Chart 2, pp. 100-103; and note your career-oriented interests [p. 52] from your SCII results)?

4. What levels of physical demands are required (compare "DOL Physical Demands," p. 53)?

5. What additional education does this option require (compare DPT, p. 56; see Educational Levels, Chart 2, pp. 100-103)?

Decision (See "Principles for Decision Making," p. 55)

_____ Acceptable   _____ Unacceptable   _____ Continue Research

Follow-through plans . . .

Career Option Evaluation Sheet

1st: WTG # _____ Career Title _____ DOT # _____

Associated Career Titles and Numbers

2nd: WTG # _____ Career Title _____ DOT # _____

3rd: WTG # _____ Career Title _____ DOT # _____

4th: WTG # _____ Career Title _____ DOT # _____

1. How does this career option fit my values (see Work Values, Chart 2, pp. 100-103; and pp. 74-75)?

2. How am I qualified by abilities, skills and gifts for this option (see Temperament, Aptitude, and Skills, Chart 2)?

3. How does this option meet my career-oriented interests (see Occupational Themes, Chart 2, pp. 100-103; and note your career-oriented interests [p. 52] from your SCII results)?

4. What levels of physical demands are required (compare "DOL Physical Demands," p. 53)?

5. What additional education does this option require (compare DPT, p. 56; see Educational Levels, Chart 2, pp. 100-103)?

Decision (See "Principles for Decision Making," p. 55)

_____ Acceptable   _____ Unacceptable   _____ Continue Research

Follow-through plans . . .

Career Option Evaluation Sheet

1st: WTG # _____ Career Title _____ DOT # _____

Associated Career Titles and Numbers

2nd: WTG # _____ Career Title _____ DOT # _____

3rd: WTG # _____ Career Title _____ DOT # _____

4th: WTG # _____ Career Title _____ DOT # _____

1. How does this career option fit my values (see Work Values, Chart 2, pp. 100-103; and pp. 74-75)?

2. How am I qualified by abilities, skills and gifts for this option (see Temperament, Aptitude, and Skills, Chart 2)?

3. How does this option meet my career-oriented interests (see Occupational Themes, Chart 2, pp. 100-103; and note your career-oriented interests [p. 52] from your SCII results)?

4. What levels of physical demands are required (compare ''DOL Physical Demands,'' p. 53)?

5. What additional education does this option require (compare DPT, p. 56; see Educational Levels, Chart 2, pp. 100-103)?

Decision (See ''Principles for Decision Making,'' p. 55)

_____ Acceptable   _____ Unacceptable   _____ Continue Research

Follow-through plans . . .

□ GROUP DISCUSSION

Purposes
□ To assist group members in clarifying career options.
□ To identify further steps for investigating career possibilities.

Discussion
1. Each member of the group share his or her views regarding the propriety of using "secular" and "sacred" categories when Christians define their careers (see p. 57).

2. Thus far, you have made a significant investment in each other's lives. Now, as members together of the body of Christ, you can serve each other by discussing career options. After all, the success of one Christian is a success for all (1 Cor. 12:26). As members of the group share their Career Options Evaluation Sheets, help each other examine the appropriateness of that career based on what you have learned about each other. Raise questions about each acceptable career option that will help clarify the follow-through that may be needed and could result in that person entering that career. The follow-through may include such things as:

Reading additional descriptive literature (see appendix C).

Aptitude testing.

More formal education, training or tutoring.

More experience—internships, externships, field work, apprenticeships, volunteer service, part-time or short-term employment.

Interviewing or corresponding with persons in that career (see appendix D).

Be certain to intersperse this activity with times of informal prayer that will allow God the opportunity to influence your interaction.

Note: When your options are being considered be sure to record the group's contributions under "Follow-through plans" at the bottom of your Career Option Evaluation Sheets.

3. Your group now has the option of deciding to complete units 13 and 14. If you decide to do these, the result of unit 13 will be a functional résumé which you will find valuable in an immediate or future job search. The value of unit 14 is having group members assist each other in developing an overall job-search plan and in refining interview skills. If you decide to complete these units, go to Looking Ahead below; if not, turn to page 97 and read and discuss the epilog. Then each person take a turn at expressing what this experience in life planning has meant personally. Also discuss future contacts with each other for encouragement in making job contacts and implementing career plans. Close with a time of prayer for each other.

Looking Ahead
Do pages 69-86 in preparation for the group's next meeting.

☐ INDIVIDUAL EXERCISE

1. Making and achieving goals defines our quality and style of life. Paul provides a good example. Read Philippians 3:12-16.
How does Paul's goal influence his evaluation of his personal progress?

His motivation?

His advice to other believers?

2. Career objectives form the hub around which all your job-search plans relate. A career objective states an occupational preference—a goal. You may develop several statements for any one career option. For example, the person who opts for a career in library services may, because of personal abilities and interests, seek employment as an aquisitions librarian or a buyer for a bookstore, or an archivist. In such an event each specific job requires a slightly different statement of objectives because each employer is different.

A well-stated objective will include either a job title or a definition of the job in terms of work activities performed. For the less experienced person, it usually identifies the entry level sought and a longer-range objective. In addition, where one wishes to be in the work world is frequently included: sector (for example, business, industry, Christian professions, social service, government), location (for example, city, state, indoors, outdoors), or organizational characteristics (for example, large company, small, prestigious, newly organized).

Sample Career Objectives

	# 1	# 2	# 3	# 4	# 5
1. Present Goal	Retail trainee	Minister of Christian education or youth	Member of production design team	Crisis counseling of youth	Accountant or assistant to controllers
2. Long-range Goal	Executive position in retail merchandising or management	Director of Christian Education in large church or state-level Christian education or youth program coordinator	(same as above)	Senior partner in a counseling center	Division controller or vice president/ Finance
3. Tasks, Skills, Competencies	Planning; organizing; supervising; buying; promoting sales; problem solving	Bible teaching; organizing youth program; song leading; camping; counseling youth; Sunday-school teacher training	Using high level mathematics in problem solving; analyzing, testing and designing products	Facilitating interpersonal adjustment; empathic listening; counseling; guiding personal problem solving	Gathering data and preparing financial reports; analyzing accounting procedures; establishing format for data processing
4. Work-Force Sector	Business: department store or chain store	Christian professions	Major industry	Private counseling services	Industrial or government accounting
5. Work Environment	No restrictions	Anywhere in USA; average to large metropolitan area	Southern states; in-service training opportunities	East coast or West coast; suburban setting	Established organization

Once you have an objective you need to decide how you can effectively inform a potential employer of your talents. Listing your qualifications will organize your personal characteristics in a way that permits you to draw on them when writing a résumé or preparing for a job interview. Your qualifications should include both the quantity and the quality of your experience and education. In reporting quantity, identify the range of duties you have performed. Quality is implied by listing the indications that you can "get the job done." Faithfulness in limited opportunities makes you a candidate for expanded responsibilities. Study the sample Stewardship Data Sheet below. Then, based on your key attributes (p. 56, #3) and the results of your Career Option Evaluation Sheets, prepare at least one Stewardship Data Sheet (pp. 71-76) and more if needed.

Stewardship Data Sheet

Career Objective

1. Present Goal *retail trainee*

2. Long-range Goal *executive, retail merchandising or management*

3. Tasks, Skills, Competencies *planning; organizing; supervising; buying; promoting sales; problem solving.*

4. Work-Force Sector *Business: department store or chain store*

5. Work Environment *no restrictions*

Qualifications (How I know I have the items listed in #3 above.)

Tasks/Skills	Quantity	Quality
Planning:	Scheduling personal time use; study plus work; junior year observation/participation project at local manufacturing firm (Blank Products); summer as Assistant party Coordinator, Big Rest Motel; Chairperson Homecoming Committee	Offered job as Coordinator of Party Service
Organizing:	Assistant party coordinator; Club leader; Student Advisory Committee Chairperson	Devised successful nature projects as Camp Counselor; was added to official leader's guide.
Supervising:	Assistant party coordinator student committees.	A in Management Course
Buying:	(No direct experience) Reviewed inventories at Blank Products	A's in Marketing and management courses.
Promoting Sales:	Assistant Party Coordinator)	A in Marketing course; saw 20% increase in repeat bookings for party services
Problem Solving:	Tutoring in accounting and algebra; handling complaints while dorm R.A.	During observation-participation at Blank Products suggested a time-saving improvement for quality control.

Stewardship Data Sheet

Career Objective

1. Present Goal

2. Long-range Goal

3. Tasks, Skills, Competencies

4. Work-Force Sector

5. Work Environment

Qualifications (How I know I have the items listed in #3 above.)

Tasks/Skills	Quantity	Quality

Stewardship Data Sheet

Career Objective

1. Present Goal

2. Long-range Goal

3. Tasks, Skills, Competencies

4. Work-Force Sector

5. Work Environment

Qualifications (How I know I have the items listed in #3 above.)

Tasks/Skills	Quantity	Quality

Stewardship Data Sheet

Career Objective

1. Present Goal

2. Long-range Goal

3. Tasks, Skills, Competencies

4. Work-Force Sector

5. Work Environment

Qualifications (How I know I have the items listed in #3 above.)

Tasks/Skills	Quantity	Quality

Stewardship Data Sheet

Career Objective

1. Present Goal

2. Long-range Goal

3. Tasks, Skills, Competencies

4. Work-Force Sector

5. Work Environment

Qualifications (How I know I have the items listed in #3 above.)

Tasks/Skills	Quantity	Quality

Stewardship Data Sheet

Career Objective

1. Present Goal

2. Long-range Goal

3. Tasks, Skills, Competencies

4. Work-Force Sector

5. Work Environment

Qualifications (How I know I have the items listed in #3 above.)

Tasks/Skills	Quantity	Quality

3. The employer knows what skills, abilities and traits are needed in an employee. You know what traits you possess. A résumé is the summary of your experience. If it is written correctly, it will inform a prospective employer about your strengths. By telling what you do and how well you do it, a good résumé will arouse an employer's interest in you.

Below is the résumé of Janice Doe, based on the sample Stewardship Data Sheet on page 71. Compare the information in the résumé with the data. Notice the use of action words and phrases by underlining them. Notice the direct and indirect ways she communicates high quality, and place a *Q* by them. Then choose three of the other sample résumés which follow, underlining action words and marking *Q* for indications of quality.

JANICE DOE

Permanent Address	Temporary Address
1001 Clinton Ave.	5726 Foster Ave.
Des Moines, IA 503XX	Chicago, IL 606XX
Telephone: 515/424-XXXX	Telephone: 312/784-XXXX

Objective   Entry position leading to a merchandising and management position in a department store handling quality products.

Qualified By   School year 19XX-XX--Selected as one of ten college residence hall assistants from a field of fifty-five applicants. Acted as a mediator between students and administration--enforcing regulations.

Summer 19XX--Received exposure to the fields of marketing, finance and higher-level management while working as an assistant to the Controller of Blank Products Corporation. Worked with auditors-- prepared charts and reviewed inventories. Successfully replaced the head of Accounts Receivable for six weeks. Worked with orders, billing, returned goods, shipping releases and special research projects.

Summer 19XX--Hired as a party coordinator with Big Rest Motel for banquets. After ten days was asked to assist my supervisor with planning and organization. Increased repeat bookings by 20%. Was offered full-time job as Director for Party Services but returned to school.

School year 19XX-XX--While participating in a cooperative education program with Blank Products Corporation observed industrial side of management and manufacturing, tested for quality control, routed orders, suggested and saw implemented improvements for greater control and accuracy while conserving time.

Education   State College, Chicago, Illinois. Candidate for B.A. degree in May 19XX, with 3.4 average (4.0=A). GPA of 4.0 in Marketing and Management courses.

One of fifteen students selected to attend Seminar in Modern Corporation in which all aspects of Service Enterprise, Inc. were studied in depth.

Activities   Elected member of State College Student Government two years. Appointed Chairperson of the 19XX Homecoming Committee, coordinating all activities. Worked with new-student orientation three years and campus blood-donation drives two years. Volunteer leader for Pioneer Girls Organization and summer day-camp for three years, devising new crafts and nature projects.

Diversions   Racquetball, swimming, sailing, needle crafts, designing clothing and interior design.

Personal Data   Birthdate: 29 June 19XX. Excellent health. Single. U.S. Citizen. Will relocate.

References   Furnished upon request.

```
RESUME FOR:    NAME
               XXXX Pine St.
               Mytown, IL  60085

               312/623-XXXX

OBJECTIVE:     Employment that will further my experience in office procedures
               with on-the-job training leading to a supervisory position.

SIGNIFICANT
   WORK
EXPERIENCES:   May 19XX to Present
               Chicago Title and Trust Co., Mytown, Illinois.
               Tract department.
               Started as a competition clerk.  Responsibilities expanded to
               working with microfilm, doing a daily report in the billing
               department and making tract searches.
               Three merit-pay evaluations have resulted in pay increases each
               time.
               Received commendations by my supervisor indicating high produc-
               tivity, helpfulness, conscientiousness, accuracy and adaptability.

               Summer 19XX
               K-Mart, Mytown, Illinois.
               Worked at the check-outs for two months.  Was at various times
               called out on the floor to straighten and stock shelves as well
               as price items.
               Received a raise after six weeks.  Awarded the top commendation,
               four stars, by K-Mart's "store shoppers" for outstanding service
               as a check-out clerk.
               Resigned because of heavy school load.

               January 19XX to June 19XX
               Anderson's Greenhouse, Mytown, Illinois.
               Responsibilities consisted of planting and selling plants.
               Pay was increased 25¢ per hour when responsibilities were in-
               creased to include sales.
               The job terminated when the spring selling season was over.

SCHOOLING:     Graduated Mytown East High School, June 19XX, with 3.66 GPA
               (A=4.0) in the honors program.

HOBBIES
   AND
INTERESTS:     Guitar playing, reading, skiing, sewing, cooking and camping.

               Membership in various musical groups including Mytown East High
               Senior Acapella Choir and church youth choir.  Member of the
               youth council at church.  Have been a member of a Bible-quiz
               team and presently teach a Sunday-school class.

PERSONAL
   DATA:       Good health.  Height:  5'1".  Weight:  105 lbs.  Birthdate:
               1-23-XX.


REFERENCES AVAILABLE UPON REQUEST.
```

DOE, JON E.

Temporary Address: Permanent Address:
Community College Box C-761   542 Ada Street
Denver, CO 80202   Anytown, MI 49855
(303) 948-XXXX   (906) 639-XXXX

Job Objective   Chief mechanic position with possible advancement to foreman
                 after on-the-job training.

Education   Community College, Denver, CO (technical school).
                 Graduated with Automotive Technician Degree in May 19XX.

                 Northern Michigan High School, Anytown, MI
                 Technical Track graduate, 19XX.

Work Experience Steel Industries, Anytown, MI (steel-treating firm).
                 Summer laborer.
                 Ran wide assortment of equipment including furnaces, drill
                 and punch presses, blastets, straighteners, saws and cranes.
                 Was advanced to heat-treating department and given raise
                 mid-July.
                 (Summer of 19XX)

                 Nukar Olds, Anytown, MI (new-car dealership).
                 Line mechanic, full time.
                 Was called on to trouble-shoot difficult electrical prob-
                 lems.
                 (19XX-XX)

                 United Parcel Service, Anytown, MI.
                 Sorter, part-time while attending school.
                 Loaded and unloaded trucks, sorted parcels.
                 Was #2 on part-time seniority list for my shift (40 workers).
                 Given informal responsibility in the supervision of my work
                 area.
                 Received favorable mention in my file for demonstrating
                 leadership and initiative.
                 (19XX-XX)

Activities   Sports, car enthusiast.

Personal   Single. Age 25. Excellent health. Will relocate.

References   Career Services/Placement
                 Community College, Denver, CO 80202.

Résumé of John Q. Doe

as of May 10, 19XX

Current Address	Box C-1501 5429 Park St. Atlanta, GA 300XX 404/288-XXXX	Permanent Address	45 Berry Blvd. Ourtown, IL 60000 312/515-XXXX

Career Objective   To obtain a management trainee position which would lead to an administrative position in domestic marketing.

Qualifications   Worked in a variety of positions for R. M. Blank Co. (19XX–XX). Hired to work in shipping department in summer of 19XX. After working for 1 month was put in charge of warehouse projects. In the summer of 19XX was put in charge of the customer services account with XYZ Inc. Worked as a trouble-shooter for two Chicago branches of R. M. Blank while in school (19XX–XX). During summer of 19XX assisted in warehouse planning and projects.

Promoted to Assistant Dealer while in college and working part-time for Name-Brand Aluminum. Achieved an 80% closing of sales over the four-year period.

In charge of a kitchen serving 300 people for two summers 19XX & 19XX at Camp Wilderness.

Named "Lifetime Honor Carrier" by the Town's Evening Record (19XX). This honor is bestowed upon carriers who give good service, solicit a substantial amount of new customers and display a good company image.

Education   City University, Atlanta, Georgia. Candidate for B.A. degree in May 19XX, with 3.32 grade average (A=4.0).

Major: Economics/Management
Minor concentration: Sociology

Dean's List last four semesters.

Extra-curricular Activities   Letterman of the Varsity Basketball Team for four years. Cocaptain one year and nominated for all-conference during the final season.

Helped organize YBA program at the North Suburban YMCA as a volunteer (19XX).

Volunteer at Senior Citizens' House in a visitation capacity during sophomore year.

Personal Data   Birthdate: March 3, 19XX.   Health: Excellent.
Marital status: Engaged.   U.S. Citizen.

References   Letters are on file and available from:
Career Services Office
City University
Atlanta, Georgia 300XX
404/945-XXXX Ext. 304

NAME
XXXX Driscoll Court
Town Park, CA 911XX
Home: 213/433-XXXX

CAREER OBJECTIVES   To use my skill and knowledge to establish myself in
helping relationships with troubled youths or adults.
To assist them in growth, problem solving and communication.

WORK EXPERIENCE   Youth Center Worker. Town Park Youth Center.
Jan. 19XX
to
Present

Organized group activities within the program; and individual outside activities; established personal relationships and counseling. Worked closely with Police Department, high-school authorities and parents. Was routinely
tapped as resource person by director.

Feb. 19XX
to
Aug. 19XX

General Office Assistant. American Library Association,
Los Angeles, California.
Varied office responsibilities. Recognized for flexibility
as supplemental personnel within three major clerical
areas: typing, computer terminal operator and correspondence.

Jan. 19XX
to
Jan. 19XX

Receptionist, General Office Assistant. Holleb, Gerstein
& Glass, Los Angeles, California.
Legal firm receptionist, answering phones, greeting clients,
running errands, using varied office skills. Part-time
during school year and in addition asked to work full-time
during the summer and vacations.

VOLUNTEER
SERVICES

Pacific Garden Mission. Counseling in the Women's Division.

"Good Samaritan" Program. Aiding elderly in various house-
hold chores.

EDUCATION   California College, B.A., Sociology, 19XX.
West Coast Bible Institute, Diploma, Bible Theology, 19XX.

PERSONAL DATA   Born: March 19, 19XX. Excellent health. Single.
Hobbies: reading, camping, variety of handcrafts.
High school: Secretary Treasurer of Junior class. Honors
in National Testing Program. Top 10% of class.
West Coast Bible Institute: Dean's List of 19XX.

REFERENCES   Upon request.

NAME
ADDRESS
TELEPHONE

Goal: To promote organizations, concepts or individuals which will make people's lives more meaningful.

Education: B.A., magna cum laude, Christian College, Boston, Mass., 19XX.
One-year postgraduate study at New England Seminary, Boston, Mass.

Work Experience: Christian College Public Relations teams (part-time).
Part-time youth pastor.
Christian College Development Department, 19XX-present.

Abilities Profile:

Organization: Developed and maintained a Special Ministries program for constituent churches. In three years the program grew to 11 public-relations teams involving 60-70 students. Responsibilities include coaching, booking, promoting, counseling and budgeting.

Instituted self-supporting summer tours for these teams.

Began a college speakers' bureau.

Development: Held major responsibility for church relations. In two years giving among constituent churches increased 20%, from $140,000 to $175,000. Work included speaking, direct-mail copy writing, and initiation of special programs and publications.

Public Relations: Admissions counselor and representative among more than 800 churches in parent denomination.
Liaison between music, admissions and development departments.
Spoke on behalf of school at more than a dozen denominational conferences.
Experience in brief or extended public speaking, extemporaneous or prepared.
Acted as trouble-shooter, handling questions and criticisms from constituents.
Attendance has increased from 3 to 30 in a college-age, Sunday-school class since I began teaching.
Spoke frequently to high-school groups about college.
Editor for one year of all college promotional literature for a total mailing list of 23,000. Responsibility for an eight-page quarterly tabloid, promotional brochures, direct-mail letters, the college news bureau.
Worked closely with in-house artist on graphic design, illustration, typography, photography and layout.
(Samples of publications available upon request.)

Personal Data:

Age: 26
Marital status: Married, no children
Health: Excellent
Honors: "Who's Who in American Colleges and Universities"
Interests: Leader of two adult musical groups; work with college-age young people

References: Available upon request.

4. Now you are ready to do a trial résumé (see pp. 84-85). Choose one of your Stewardship Data Sheets as the basis for your résumé. Remember, your goal is to present your strengths in a manner that will arouse an employer's interest in you. So, use action words such as *generated, proposed, analyzed, created, reorganized, set up, improved*. Work, volunteer and educational experiences are always listed from most recent to least recent. References may be handled in three ways: (1) "On file with . . . ," (2) "Available upon request" or (3) a list of two to four persons and their addresses. (*Always* contact references in advance to ask if you may use their names.)

Make it flow—brief enough to be read, words enough to communicate. Add, delete, combine or retitle paragraphs or sections in accordance with your preference and uniqueness. Some persons find that titles such as "Selected Work Experiences," "Qualifications Profile," "Significant Experiences," or "Summary" are easier to use than complete chronological listings under "Work Experiences" and "Education." Creativity is not only okay, but even desirable, so long as it makes clear to the employer why *you* should be employed.

Trial Résumé

Name

Address

Telephone

Career Objective

Qualified By
or
Work Experiences

Education

Personal Data

Activities

References

If possible get photocopies of your Trial Résumé and its Stewardship Data Sheet to distribute for your group discussion. If you had several Data Sheets, you may wish to complete additional résumés.

□ GROUP DISCUSSION

Purposes
□ To evaluate and strengthen each group member's Trial Résumé.
□ To provide each group member with a résumé that can actually be used in a job search.

Discussion
1. Each person share some thought about Paul's use of goals or some personal practice in goal setting that was influenced as a result of studying Paul's example.
2. Each person share one of his or her Stewardship Data Sheets and Trial Résumés. Ask clarifying questions. Suggest modifications. Give the assistance each person requests in editing and rewriting.

Looking Forward
Do the individual exercise on pages 87-94 in preparation for your next group meeting.

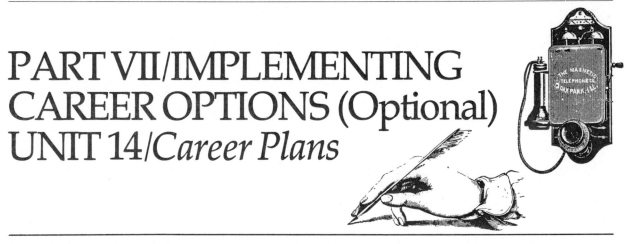

PART VII/IMPLEMENTING CAREER OPTIONS (Optional)
UNIT 14/*Career Plans*

☐ INDIVIDUAL EXERCISE

You must design a strategy for finding job vacancies in your chosen career. In this unit we will discuss job-search plans and the tools you will use. The exercises to follow will help you practice some of the search skills you need.

There are two main approaches to a job search. The more traditional approach is to send a résumé and letter of application to an organization's personnel recruiter; if qualified, being asked to come for a screening interview; if a good candidate, going through further interviewing and evaluation by a department head you would work for; if best qualified, offered a job.

The second job-search approach is the field survey, which is a "who you know" approach. You begin by chatting with every person who shows the slightest interest in the same kind of career objectives you have. You find out who they know who shares your same enthusiasms and interests, and then get in touch with those persons. Again, you ask these people who else you might talk to, and so on. You do not discuss a job directly, rather you discuss the characteristics of and the need for excellent people in, for example, counseling or sales/marketing. You ask what problems and frustrations are faced by persons in these areas. As your information base expands and your contacts widen, you will soon become acquainted with people whom you could come back to with a job proposal indicating how employing you could help solve their problems or make a profit for their company or organization. *Very important:* when doing a field survey, do not make actual job proposals and, if offered a job, ask for time to complete your survey before making a decision. A Field Survey Simulation will be one of your activities in this unit.

There are many details not discussed here. Browsing through one or two of the publications listed in appendix E will help you; especially useful are the books by Bolles and Powell.

Some of the tools you will need in addition to your résumé include records, information about the employer and communication techniques. Decide how you are going to keep records on potential employers. Some people have one large chart with all contacts listed. Others use a folder for each prospect. One compromise is a notebook with a section for each employer. Your strategy sheet for the employers might look something like the one on page 89.

There is much information available about an organization and the business trends it and others like it are experiencing. (See references listed in appendix D.) Obtaining the following kinds of information can aid your decision making as well as your interview since you get that far:

Comparative size.   Number and location of offices, stores or plants.
Potential for expansion.   Financial picture—profits, assets, stock.
Growth over past three to five years.   Opportunities for moving up.

Diversification of products or services. Patterns of progression.
New services or products being developed. Current publicity.
Attention given to evaluation & development. Salary range.

The more of this information you have before a field survey or job interview the better. Once you are on site you may ask questions to complete your profile on that organization.

Some of the things you should probably ask about are affected by the quality of leadership in the organization. As a Christian, you may be particularly interested in the following:

Servant-style leadership. (Read Mt. 23:1-11 and Mk. 10:42-45.)[15]

Distribution of power. (Is everyone in the organization important, encouraged to grow and rewarded equitably?)

Shared decision making. (Is everyone who is affected by a decision included in substantial ways into the making of the decision?)

Salaries based on equity and need. (Are they at least influenced by these principles?)

Institutional lifestyle. (Is it concerned with conservation of nonrenewable resources, sharing of human resources or socially responsible investment of financial resources?)

Institutional alliance with, or at least commitment to, the poor and the oppressed. (Read Ezek. 16:49).

Think through your communication skills. You will practice interview skills with your group. For telephone communications, the following may help:

Write out the purpose of your call ahead of time.

List main points to be communicated.

Obtain the name of the person who can give you the information or who needs to know your qualifications.

Let that person know she or he is special—you have sought him or her out purposely.

Usually, he or she will be interested in you because helping you can help his or her organization.

Keep the contact brief and friendly.

The other main skill is letter writing. There are several types of letters. You will find one example on page 90 and others in the reference materials listed in appendix D. The types of letters include:

Inquiry. (See p. 90) Appreciation
Application (a variation of the inquiry). —for information.
Confirmation —for time spent with you.
—of telephone conversation. —for hosting you at on-site interview.
—of appointment. —as a means of reminding an employer of your
—of details in job offer. continuing interest.
—of acceptance. Informing other employers you have accepted
—of declining an offer. employment elsewhere.

In all your correspondence, put yourself in the other person's shoes and use that as the basis for your approach—the Golden Rule.

Filling Out a Contact Strategy Sheet

Prepare a sheet for each company or organization you decide to contact.

You may wish to note the source of information. How you obtained this name, such as *College Placement Annual,* page XX or Sam Jones, (friend of a neighbor) and so on.

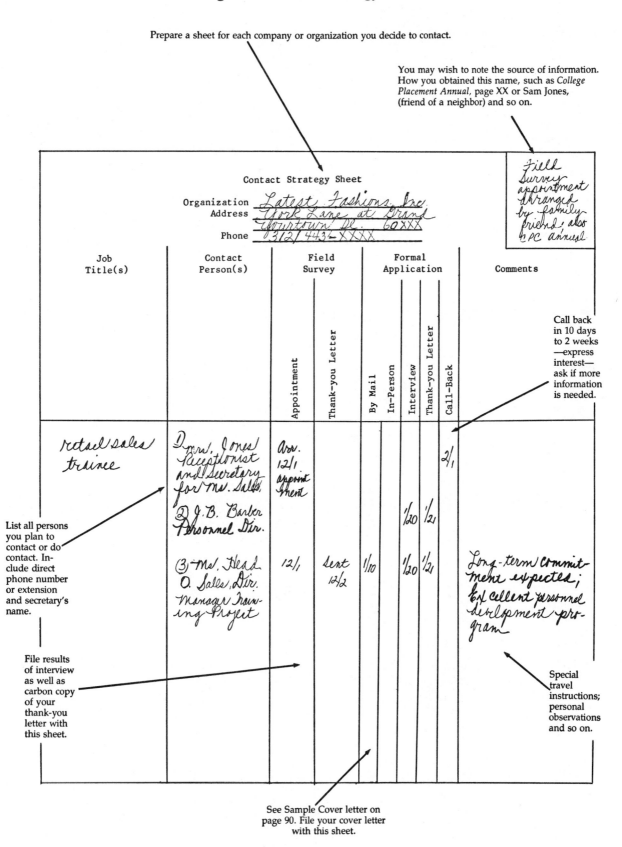

Contact Strategy Sheet

Organization *Latest Fashions, Inc.*
Address *York Lane at Grand*
Yourtown, Ill.   60XXX
Phone *312/ 443- XXXX*

Field Survey appointment arranged by family friend; also CPC annual.

Job Title(s)	Contact Person(s)	Field Survey		Formal Application				Comments
		Appointment	Thank-you Letter	By Mail	In-Person	Interview	Thank-you Letter	Call-Back	

Call back in 10 days to 2 weeks —express interest— ask if more information is needed.

retail sales trainee — ① *Mrs. Jones Receptionist and Secretary for Mrs. Sales.* — Appointment: *arr. 12/1 appointment* — Call-Back: *2/1*

② *J.B. Barber Personnel Dir.* — Interview: *1/20* — Thank-you Letter: *1/21*

③ *Ms. Head O. Sales, Dir. Manager Training Project* — Appointment: *12/1* — Thank-you Letter (Field Survey): *Sent 12/2* — By Mail: *1/10* — Interview: *1/20* — Thank-you Letter: *1/21* — Comments: *Long-term commitment expected; Excellent personnel development program*

List all persons you plan to contact or do contact. Include direct phone number or extension and secretary's name.

File results of interview as well as carbon copy of your thank-you letter with this sheet.

Special travel instructions; personal observations and so on.

See Sample Cover letter on page 90. File your cover letter with this sheet.

Sample Cover Letter

When you are unable to apply for a job in person, your résumé should always be sent with a covering letter. Here is a sample.

Businesslike stationery. It is all right to use colored or textured paper.

Individually typed, neat, original copy.

Janice Doe
5726 Foster Ave.
Chicago, IL 600XX
Home 312/784-XXXX
January 10, 19XX

Where you can be reached.

Correct name, position, address— correctly spelled.

Ms. Hed O. Sales
Director
Manager Training Project
Latest Fashions, Inc.
Yourtown, IL 60XXX

Use plain English— no gimmicks.

Salutation addressee prefers.

Dear Ms. Sales:

Key qualifications— friendly but not flippant.

Do you have an opening for a sales representative? I will complete a B.A. in Economics/Management at State College, Chicago, Illinois in May.

Reason for writing.

I have had direct experience in the fields of marketing and management in my summer employment opportunities. My extra-curricular and volunteer service experiences have strength-ened my skills in the areas of planning, organizing and supervising. I made a positive contribution in each of my part-time employment situations.

Your personal interest in them.

The 20% increase in repeat bookings for party services at Big Rest Motels convinced me that marketing excites me. Your advertisement in the College Placement Annual that explains your retail trainee program prompted me to write you. I aspire to a management position in merchandising.

I am enclosing my resume which only gives the highlights of my qualifications. I hope I will have the opportunity to discuss my credentials with you personally. Since I am only 30 miles away I am available for an interview at your convenience.

Invite response.

Thank you for your time and consideration.

Polite close.

Sincerely yours,

Personally signed.

Janice Doe

Janice Doe

The résumé is enclosure.

Enclosure

Double check spelling and grammar.

1. The first activity will help you learn more about your career interest and interview skills. In this case you will do the interviewing rather than being interviewed. Select one person who is working at a job in one of your career options. Since most people like to talk about their work, you should find it easy to arrange an appointment. Use the following form. It is okay to take notes during the interview.

Field Survey
1. In regard to your career, what aspects interest or excite you most?

2. How did you develop these interests?

3. What were your most helpful experiences before you took this job?

4. What do you do in a typical day? problems? decisions?

5. What aspects of your career give you the most satisfaction?

6. What frustrations or dissatisfactions do you have in your career?

7. What does it take to do your job well?

8. What are the major job levels in your occupation? How does one progress?

9. How is this career field changing?

10. Are there social obligations? organizations you must join or required after-hours activities?

11. How are you informed of the quality of your contribution? How are you rewarded?

12. Does working here make you feel valued and important? Why or why not?

13. Are you informed about decisions that will affect you before they are made? Explain.

14. How are the leaders in your organization accountable to those they serve?

15. How are salaries at the various levels of the organization determined?

16. Is the organization primarily concerned with its own preservation? Explain.

17. Have you any advice for persons interested in getting into this profession?

18. Can you put me in touch with someone else who could share information on this profession?

19. (Other questions)

2. Be sure to send a thank-you note to the person you interviewed. Mention significant information you gained.

Now, try to get in touch with the feelings you had during the interview. What were they? How do they influence your attitude toward this occupational option?

3. During your group meeting you will take turns being interviewed by each other. To prepare for that, review your Stewardship Data Sheets (pp. 72-76) and fill in the items below.

Preinterview Planning

1. My major strengths are...

2. My major weaknesses are...
(Note: Be honest. Usually a weakness implies a strength, so present it in that light. For example: "As a reference librarian I read incessantly and have to force myself to get enough physical exercise.")

3. I plan to use my previous experience in my career by...

4. I am seeking employment now because...
(Note: Avoid criticism of former employers; the change is an opportunity for growth.)

5. Persons who can tell you more about me are...
(Note: Persons who know your competence, character, personality and special attributes, especially as an employee.)

6. My long-term career goal, say ten years from now is...

7. My avocational interests include . . .

8. Am I applying to other companies?
(Note: It may help an interested interviewer to give you an early decision if you indicate you are interviewing elsewhere.)

9. If I were given the opportunity to work for your organization, I would be able to . . .
(Note: Research the organization ahead of time to see where you can be of most help to them.)

10. The salary range I am expecting is . . .
(Note: Check the salary surveys done by the U.S. Dept. of Labor or the College Placement Council, and place your expectation on the above average to high side.)

11. When my life is over, I should like to be remembered for . . .

You will be role-playing an actual interview at your group meeting, so prepare for that discussion as if you were going for an interview. Have these notes clearly in mind. Dress appropriately and neatly. Watch your personal hygiene—hair, teeth, breath, fingernails and so on.

4. Keep the faith. One of the more difficult aspects to a job search is rejection. When many contacts have been made and some have led to the interview stage but no job offer has been made, one can begin doubting oneself. A Christian has an added advantage in battling discouragement.

Read Hebrews 10:15-16. What can God's influence in one's life mean when the temptation to doubt one's choices presents itself?

Read John 14:27 and Philippians 4:4-7. How can one keep peace of heart in times of discouragement?

□ GROUP DISCUSSION

Purposes
□ To improve interview skills.
□ To build confidence in plans for implementing career strategies.
□ To give opportunity for long-term commitment to providing encouragement for each group member.

Discussion
1. Each person tell about his or her Field Survey interview. How did it go? What did you learn? How did you feel?

Explore with each person how he or she might use this technique in a career plan. Suggest additional contacts, if possible.

2. To practice being interviewed for a job, each member play the roles of interviewee and employer. Other group members observe the interviewee and take notes to be shared later. There are questions below for the "employer" to ask. There is also a rating chart to guide the "observers." Before beginning, each interviewee should indicate what general category of career he or she is interviewing for.

Recent research indicates that of the ten characteristics employers look for, only intelligence is communicated in one's verbal behavior. The other nine, such things as ability to communicate, motivation, initiative, confidence and personality, are judged largely on the basis of the candidate's nonverbal behavior. The most important times to be sociable are the first two and the last five minutes of the interview. But even if you start slow it is essential to end strong.

After your role play, the "employer" should first discuss your nonverbal patterns, followed by the observers. Be sure to take notes on their comments. It is okay to give the interviewer feedback on his or her mannerisms too.

You should avoid putting on an act in the interview, but find ways to be authentic in your nonverbal behavior. Being certain of your career goals, realistically assessing yourself, anticipating the interview questions and being ready to suggest how you might be a specific asset in the interviewer's organization are good preparation.

Questions for Job Interview Simulation

In what school activities have you participated? Why? Which did you enjoy the most?

What courses did you like best? Least? Why?

How much money do you hope to earn at age 30? 50?

What do you think determines a person's progress in a good company or organization?

Are you primarily interested in making money, or do you feel that service to others is a satisfactory accomplishment?

Tell me about yourself.

What interests you about our product or service?

Have you ever changed your major field of interest? Why?

When did you choose your academic major?

If you were given a chance to work for our organization, how do you think you could be of most value to us?

Why did you choose your school?

Why did you think you might like to work for our company?

Do you think that your extracurricular activities were worth the time devoted to them? Why?

Would you prefer a large or a small organization? Why?

Are you willing to go where an employer sends you?

What is your major weakness?

Which of your college years was the most difficult? Why?

Have you ever had any difficulty getting along with fellow students or faculty?

What kind of boss do you prefer?

How do you feel about your family?

How do you spend your spare time? What are your hobbies?

Do more practice interviews on your own. Ask a friend to help you by playing interviewer and giving feedback.

3. Have a time of sharing in which the responses to the Scripture passages on peace of heart are discussed (p. 94).

How can one's relationships in the body of Christ be used to implement these principles?
4. Now turn to page 97 and read and discuss the epilog. Each person then take a turn at expressing what this group experience in life planning has meant personally. Also discuss future contacts with each other for encouragement in making job contacts and implementing career plans. Close with a time of prayer for each other.

Observer's Notes on Preferred Nonverbal Behavior

Rate on a scale of 0 (low) to 10 (high)

General comments for...	Dress, hygiene—clean? neat? appropriate?	Eye contact—how steady?	Smiles—pleasant face?	Forward-leaning posture?	Meaningful gestures?	Distinct speech?	Voice—pleasant? modulated? expressive?
Candidate #1							
Candidate #2							
Candidate #3							
Candidate #4							

How I was rated

Note
[15]Two excellent references are R. K. Greenleaf, *Servant Leadership: A Journey into the Nature of Legitimate Power & Greatness* (Paramus, N.J.: Paulist-Newman Press, 1977), and L. O. Richards and C. Hoeldtke, *A Theology of Church Leadership* (Grand Rapids, Mich.: Zondervan, 1980).

EPILOG

You have learned a great deal about yourself in the last few months as you have worked through this book. We would caution you, however, not to sit back and assume that your values, abilities and interests will not shift or grow. Remember that God will continue to change you over time as you follow his leading in the vocational as well as in the other areas of your life. It could therefore be helpful to periodically update your responses in various sections of the book. For example, after a period of significant growth in values or skill development, you could turn to the individual exercises in those units and rethink your responses. Follow through on the changes by recording them in unit 11 and on your Guide sheet. You might date your changes too. Finally, discover the meaning of these changes by checking the new information against the charts in appendix A.

Most importantly, you have learned how to relate to other Christians in ways that will appropriately *further your career*. Perhaps you will not repeat the exercises in this book, but we hope you will involve the group of believers you are most naturally a part of in a similar process. Perhaps with the support of a Christian community you will carry through on the career decisions you made while completing this book. Or perhaps you will again use the process you learned of involving a group of believers when making a future career decision.

Whatever happens, we would like to remind you in closing that your calling is to seek first the kingdom of God. As you discover and clarify your ever-developing vocational skills with the help of a body of believers, you will be more likely to relate the occupation you choose to the needs of others, and thus *further the kingdom*. "Your career" will more accurately be your kingdom calling—not a personal possession, but service to others.

APPENDIX A
Bridges to Careers in General

Chart 1. Relating Academic Interests and Occupational Themes to Occupational Interest Groups

Education or Training	Worker Trait Group Numbers	Occupational Themes
Accounting	07.01; 07.02; 07.03; 07.05; 07.06; 08.01; 11.01; 11.02; 11.06	C
Agricultural Business	03.03; 08.01; 08.02; 08.03; 11.02; 11.06; 11.07; 11.10; 11.11	E
Agricultural Production	02.02; 02.03; 02.04; 03.01; 03.02 03.03; 03.04; 04.01; 04.02; 05.01; 05.07; 08.01; 11.07; 11.10	R
Agricultural Services	02.02; 02.03; 03.01; 03.02; 03.03; 03.04; 04.01; 04.02; 05.01; 05.04; 05.07; 05.08; 08.01; 11.07; 11.10; 11.12	R
Air Conditioning and Refrigeration	05.05; 05.06; 05.10; 06.02; 06.03; 11.07	R
Algebra	02.01; 02.02; 02.04; 05.01; 05.03; 05.05; 05.06; 05.07; 08.02; 10.01; 11.01; 11.02; 11.03; 11.07	I
Art—Studio Art/ Arts and Crafts	01.01; 01.02; 01.03; 01.05; 01.06; 01.07; 08.02; 09.01; 10.01; 10.02; 11.02; 11.07	A
Automotive Services and Diesel	05.01; 05.05; 05.07; 05.10; 05.12; 06.01; 06.02; 06.03; 11.07; 11.12; 12.01	R
Biological Sciences	02.01; 02.02; 02.03; 02.04; 03.01; 03.02; 03.03; 03.04; 05.01; 05.05; 06.02; 06.03; 07.05; 08.02; 10.01; 10.02; 11.02; 11.07; 11.10	I
Chemistry	02.01; 02.02; 02.03; 02.04; 05.01; 05.03; 05.05; 06.02; 06.03; 08.02; 10.01; 11.02; 11.07; 11.10	I
Child Care	08.02; 09.01; 10.01; 10.03; 11.02; 11.07	E
Commercial Art	01.02; 01.06; 08.02; 08.03; 11.02; 11.09	A
Communications	01.01; 01.02; 01.03; 01.06; 02.04; 05.01; 08.02; 11.02; 11.04; 11.08; 11.09	A
Construction	05.05; 05.10; 05.11; 06.02; 06.03; 11.07	R
Construction & Maintenance	05.03; 05.05; 05.07; 05.08; 05.09; 05.10; 05.11; 05.12; 11.07	R
Consumer and Homemaking	01.08; 05.12; 06.01; 06.02; 08.02; 09.04; 09.05; 10.01; 10.03; 11.02	E

Education or Training	Worker Trait Group Numbers	Occupational Themes
Data Processing	07.02; 07.05; 07.06; 08.01; 11.01; 11.02	C
Dental Technology	02.02; 02.04; 05.05; 07.04; 07.05; 08.01; 10.02; 10.03; 11.02; 11.07	S
Drafting	05.01; 05.03; 05.05; 05.07; 05.10; 06.01; 06.02; 06.03; 08.01; 11.07	R
Drama	01.01; 01.02; 01.03; 01.04; 01.05 01.07; 08.02; 09.01; 10.01; 10.02 11.02; 11.07; 11.08	A
Earth Sciences	02.01; 02.04; 05.01; 05.03; 05.11; 08.02; 10.01; 11.02; 11.03; 11.07; 11.10	I
Electrical/ Electronic	05.01; 05.03; 05.05; 05.06; 05.07; 05.09; 05.10; 05.12; 06.01; 06.02; 06.03; 11.07	R
Energy/Power Systems— Professional	02.01; 02.04; 05.01; 05.06; 08.02; 11.02; 11.10	I
Energy/Power Systems— Technological	05.03; 05.05; 05.07; 05.10; 11.07	R
Finance	07.01; 07.02; 07.03; 07.04; 07.05; 08.01; 11.02; 11.05; 11.06; 11.11; 11.12	E
Food Management	02.02; 05.05; 05.10; 05.12; 06.02; 06.04; 07.01; 07.06; 09.04; 09.05; 11.02; 11.05; 11.11	E
Foreign Languages	08.02; 10.01; 11.02; 11.03; 11.08; 11.09	A
Furnishings— Clothings, Textiles and Home	05.10; 06.01; 06.02; 06.04; 08.02; 09.04; 11.02; 11.07; 11.11	E
General Clerical	05.09; 05.10; 05.12; 06.02; 07.01; 07.02; 07.03; 07.04; 07.05; 07.06; 07.07; 08.01; 11.02; 11.06	C
General Merchandising	05.10; 07.03; 08.01; 08.02; 08.03 09.04; 11.02; 11.05; 11.06; 11.09; 11.11; 11.12	E
Geography	02.01; 02.02; 07.04; 07.05; 08.02; 10.01; 11.02; 11.03; 11.07	S
Geometry	02.01; 02.02; 02.04; 05.01; 05.03; 05.05; 05.06; 05.07; 08.02; 10.01; 11.01; 11.02; 11.03; 11.07	I

Education or Training	Worker Trait Group Numbers	Occupational Themes
Government—Administration	11.04; 11.05; 11.06; 11.09	E
Government—Enforcement	04.01; 06.03; 11.10; 11.12	R
Government—Theory	11.02; 11.03; 11.07; 11.08	I
Graphic Art	01.02; 01.06; 08.02; 08.03; 11.02; 11.09	A
Health	02.01; 02.02; 02.03; 02.04; 05.05; 06.02; 06.03; 08.02; 10.01; 10.02; 10.03; 11.02; 11.07; 11.10	I
History	08.01; 08.02; 09.01; 10.01; 11.02; 11.03; 11.04; 11.07; 11.08	S
Language Skills	01.01; 02.03; 08.02; 10.01; 11.08	A
Literature	01.01; 08.02; 11.02; 11.03; 11.08	A
Management—Institutional and Home	05.10; 05.12; 10.03; 11.02; 11.05; 11.07; 11.11	E
Manufacturing/Production	02.01; 02.04; 05.01; 05.03; 05.05; 05.06; 05.09; 05.10; 05.11; 05.12; 06.01; 06.02; 06.03; 06.04; 11.05 11.07; 11.10; 11.12	R
Marketing	05.10; 07.03; 08.01; 08.02; 08.03; 09.04; 11.02; 11.05; 11.06; 11.09; 11.11; 11.12	E
Math—Advanced	02.01; 02.02; 02.04; 05.01; 05.03; 08.02; 10.01; 11.01; 11.02; 11.03; 11.07; 11.10	I
Math—Basic Skills	03.01; 05.03; 05.05; 05.06; 05.07; 05.09; 06.01; 07.02; 07.03; 08.02; 10.01; 11.02; 11.06; 11.07; 11.10	I
Mechanics	03.04; 05.05; 05.10; 06.02; 06.07; 11.07	R
Medical Technology	02.02; 02.04; 05.05; 07.04; 07.05; 08.01; 10.02; 10.03; 11.02; 11.07	S
Metalworking	02.01; 05.01; 05.05; 05.07; 05.10; 05.12; 06.01; 06.02; 06.03; 06.04; 11.07	R
Music	01.01; 01.02; 01.03; 01.04; 01.05; 08.02; 10.01; 10.02; 11.02; 11.03; 11.07	A
Nursing Care	08.01; 10.02; 10.03; 11.02; 11.07	S
Personal Services	08.02; 08.03; 09.02; 09.05; 10.02; 10.03; 11.02; 11.11	S
Photography	01.02; 01.06; 08.02; 08.03; 11.02; 11.09	A
Physical Education	04.01; 04.02; 10.02; 10.03; 11.07; 11.12; 12.01; 12.02	R
Physics	02.01; 02.02; 02.03; 02.04; 05.01; 05.03; 05.04; 06.02; 06.03; 08.02; 10.01; 10.02; 10.03; 11.01; 11.02; 11.07	I
Product Services	05.01; 05.05; 05.10; 11.07; 11.12	R
Psychology	04.01; 04.02; 07.01; 07.04; 08.01; 08.02; 09.01; 10.01; 10.02; 10.03; 11.02; 11.03; 11.07; 11.10	S
Repair—Appliance/Small Engine	05.05; 05.10; 05.12; 06.02; 06.03; 11.07	R
Restaurant—Processed Foods	02.02; 05.05; 05.09; 05.10; 05.12; 06.01; 06.02; 06.04; 09.04; 09.05; 11.07; 11.10	R
Sales and Services	07.01; 07.03; 07.04; 07.05; 08.01; 08.02; 08.03; 09.01; 09.03; 09.04; 09.05; 11.02; 11.05; 11.07; 11.09; 11.11; 11.12	E
Secretarial and Typing	07.01; 07.02; 07.05; 07.06; 08.01; 11.02	C
Sociology	04.01; 04.02; 07.01; 07.04; 08.01; 08.02; 09.01; 10.01; 10.02; 10.03; 11.02; 11.03; 11.07; 11.10	S
Space Sciences	02.01; 02.04; 05.01; 05.03; 05.11; 08.02; 10.01; 11.02; 11.03; 11.07; 11.10	I
Speech	01.03; 01.07; 08.02; 10.01; 10.02; 11.02; 11.04; 11.08	A
Textile/Leather/Upholstering	05.03; 05.05; 05.09; 06.01; 06.02; 06.03; 06.05; 09.04	R
Transportation	05.03; 05.05; 09.03	R
Woodworking	02.02; 05.05; 05.10; 06.02; 06.03; 06.04	R

Chart 2. Relating Occupational Interest Groups to Personal Characteristics

Legend for DOL Aptitude Areas (p. 52): H = Highly Skilled or Above Average · A = Average · M = Below Average or Least Skilled

WTG No.	Worker Trait Group	Occupational Themes (p. 52) R I A S E C	DOL Temperament Code (p. 51) 1 2 3 4 5 6 7 8 9 0 X Y	DOL Work Values (p. 51) 1 2 3 4 5 6 7 8 9 0	Adaptive Skills (p. 51) 1 2 3 4 5 6 7 8 9 10 11 12 13 14 15	DOL Aptitude Areas (p. 52) G V N S P Q K F M E C	Ed. Lv. (p. 53) from–to
01.	**Artistic**						
01.01	Literary Arts	. i A s . .	. . . × × . × × × . × .	. . . . × × . × . .	. . × . . × . . × . × × × . .	H H	T/G
01.02	Visual Arts	r i A s . .	× . . × . × . . × . × .	. . . . × × . × . .	. . × . . . . . × . × × . . .	A . . H H . A A A . H	T/G
01.03	Performing Arts: Drama	. i A s e .	. . . × × . . × × . × .	. . . . × × . × . .	. × × × × . . × × . × × × × .	A H . . . . A H A A .	T/G
01.04	Performing Arts: Music	. i A s e .	. . . × × . . × × . × ×	. . . . × × . × . .	. × × . . . . × × . × × × × .	H H A A A A A H H H .	T/G
01.05	Performing Arts: Dance	r . A s e .	. . . × × . . × × . × .	. . . . × × . × . .	. . × . . . × . × . × × × × .	A H . A A . A A . H .	H/G
01.06	Craft Arts	R i A s e .	. . . . × . . . × . × .	. . . . . ×	. . . . × × × . × × × × × . .	A . . A A A A A A . A	H/G
01.07	Elemental Arts	. . A s E .	. . . . × . . . × . × .	. . . . . ×	. × × × . . × × × . × × × . ×	A A M A . . M . A M A	H/G
01.08	Modeling	. . A s e .	× . × . × . . . × . × .	× ×	. × × . . . × . × . × . × . ×	A A A . . . A . A . .	H/T
02.	**Scientific**						
02.01	Physical Sci.	R I a s e .	. . . × × . × × × × . ×	× . . × × × × × . .	. . × . . × × × × . × × × . .	H H H H H A A A A . A	C/G
02.02	Life Sciences	R I . s . .	. . . . × . . × × × . ×	× . . . . . × × . .	. . × . . × × × × . × × × . .	H H H H H A A A A . A	C/G
02.03	Medical Sciences	r I a s e .	. . . . × . . × × × . ×	. . . × . . × . . .	. . . . × × × × × . × × × . .	H H H H H . . H . . A	C/G
02.04	Laboratory Technology	r I . s . c	. . . . × × × ×	. . . . . . × . . .	× . . . . × . . × . × × × . .	A H A A H A A A A . A	T/G
03.	**Plants & Animals**						
03.01	Managerial Work: Plants & Animals	R i a s e c	. . . × × . . × × × . .	× × . . . . . . × ×	. × . × × × . . × . × . × . ×	A A A A M A M A A M M	T/G

*For in-depth information on Occupational Themes see G.O.E., appendix A, p. 325, and J. L. Holland, *Making Vocational Choices: A Theory of Careers.* (Englewood Cliffs, N.J.: Prentice-Hall, 1973).

03.02	General Supervision: Plants & Animals
03.03	Animal Training & Service
03.04	Elemental Work: Plants & Animals
04.	**Protective**
04.01	Safety — Law Enforcement
04.02	Security Services
05.	**Mechanical**
05.01	Engineering
05.02	Managerial Work: Mechanical
05.03	Engineering Technology
05.04	Air & Water Vehicle Operation
05.05	Craft Technology
05.06	Systems Operation
05.07	Quality Control
05.08	Land & Water Vehicle Operation
05.09	Materials Control
05.10	Crafts
05.11	Equipment Operation
05.12	Elemental Work: Mechanical
06.	**Industrial**
06.01	Production Technology
06.02	Production Work
06.03	Quality Control
06.04	Elemental Work: Industrial

Legend (DOL Aptitude Areas, p. 52):
H = Highly Skilled or Above Average
A = Average
M = Below Average or Least Skilled

Column groups: Ed. Lv. (p. 53) · DOL Aptitude Areas (p. 52): C, E, M, F, K, Q, P, S, N, V, G · Adaptive Skills (p. 51): 15 Leads Wisely, 14 Shows Empathy, 13 Disciplined, 12 Accepts Self, 11 Responsible, 10 Respects Authority, 9 Resourceful/Creative Problem Solver, 8 Purposeful/Goal Directed, 7 Open to Change, 6 Objective/Sees Both Sides, 5 Relates Honesty, 4 Friendly, 3 Enjoys Keeping Busy, 2 Dresses Appropriately, 1 Conscientious · DOL Work Values (p. 51): 0 Tangible Pay-Off, 9 Technical Advances, 8 Creative-Abstract, 7 Technical or Scientific Activities, 6 Communication with People, 5 Reward of Prestige, 4 Social Improvement, 3 Routine-Concrete, 2 Business Activities, 1 Dealing with Objects · DOL Temperament Code (p. 51): Y Precise Attainment of Standards, X Interpretation/Personal Viewpoint, 0 Measurable or Verifiable Criteria, 9 Sensory or Judgmental Criteria, 8 Performing under Stress/Taking Risks, 7 Influencing People, 6 Working Alone, 5 Dealing with People/Team Effort, 4 Planning/Being in Control, 3 Given Specific Instructions, 2 Repetition/Standard Procedures, 1 Variety of Duties/Changes · Occupational Themes (p. 52): R, I, A, S, E, C

DOL Aptitude Areas

Worker Trait Group	Ed. Lv.	C	E	M	F	K	Q	P	S	N	V	G
07. Business Detail												
07.01 Administrative Detail	O/C				A		A			A	A	A
07.02 Mathematical Detail	O/T		A		A		A			A	A	A
07.03 Financial Detail	O/T				A	A	A			A	A	A
07.04 Oral Communications	O/C			A		A	A			A	A	A
07.05 Records Processing	O/T				A		A			A	A	A
07.06 Clerical Machine Operation	O/T			A	A	A	A	A		M	M	M
07.07 Clerical Handling	O			A	A	A	A	A		A	A	A
08. Selling												
08.01 Sales Technology	T/G						A			A	H	H
08.02 General Sales	O/T						A			A	A	A
08.03 Vending	O			A	A		A			A	A	M
09. Accommodating												
09.01 Hospitality Services	O/T						M			A	A	A
09.02 Barber & Beauty Services	O/T	A	A	A	A	H	A	A	A		A	A
09.03 Passenger Services	O/T		A	A		A	A			A	A	A
09.04 Customer Services	O			A	M	A	A			A	A	A
09.05 Attendant Services	O	M		A	M	A	A	M	M	A	A	A

Adaptive Skills (× = applies)

Worker Trait Group	15	14	13	12	11	10	9	8	7	6	5	4	3	2	1
07.01				×	×	×	×		×		×	×	×	×	
07.02			×		×	×		×		×	×	×	×	×	
07.03			×		×	×		×			×	×	×	×	
07.04			×	×	×	×			×		×	×	×	×	×
07.05					×								×	×	×
07.06			×		×	×					×	×	×	×	×
07.07			×		×						×	×			
08.01	×		×	×	×		×	×	×		×	×	×	×	
08.02	×		×	×	×		×	×	×		×	×	×	×	
08.03		×	×	×	×				×		×	×			
09.01		×			×					×	×	×			
09.02				×	×		×	×	×		×	×		×	
09.03						×	×		×		×	×			×
09.04						×	×				×	×		×	×
09.05		×	×		×	×	×	×			×	×		×	×

DOL Work Values (× = applies)

Worker Trait Group	0	9	8	7	6	5	4	3	2	1
07.01					×				×	
07.02		×						×	×	×
07.03					×			×	×	×
07.04		×			×				×	×
07.05					×			×	×	×
07.06		×						×	×	×
07.07								×	×	×
08.01	×			×	×	×	×		×	×
08.02	×				×				×	
08.03					×			×	×	×
09.01			×		×	×	×		×	
09.02		×	×		×	×				
09.03								×	×	×
09.04						×		×	×	×
09.05						×		×	×	×

DOL Temperament Code (× = applies)

Worker Trait Group	Y	X	0	9	8	7	6	5	4	3	2	1
07.01	×		×	×				×				×
07.02	×		×				×				×	
07.03	×		×					×				
07.04	×		×	×				×		×		×
07.05	×		×				×	×		×	×	
07.06	×		×				×			×		
07.07			×									
08.01			×	×	×	×		×	×			
08.02				×		×		×				
08.03						×		×				
09.01	×			×				×	×			×
09.02			×	×				×				×
09.03			×	×				×		×		
09.04								×				×
09.05								×		×	×	

Occupational Themes

Worker Trait Group	R	I	A	S	E	C
07.01			a	S	e	C
07.02		i		s	e	C
07.03		i		s	e	C
07.04		i		s	e	C
07.05		i		s	e	C
07.06	r	i		s	e	C
07.07	r			s	e	C
08.01	r			s	E	c
08.02	r	i		S	E	c
08.03		i	a	s	E	c
09.01	r		a	S	e	c
09.02	r		a	S	e	c
09.03	R			S	e	c
09.04	r			S	e	c
09.05	r			S	e	c

10.	**Humanitarian**																																															
10.01	Social Services		i	a	S			x		x	x				x					x	x	x		x				x	x		x	x	x	x		.	x		x	x		x		H	H	A		T/G
10.02	Nursing, Therapy & Specialized Teaching Services	r	i	a	S			x		x		x		x	x			x		x	x			x				x		x	x	x		x	x	x		x	x	A	A	A	A	A	A	A	A	A		A	T/G
10.03	Child & Adult Care	r	i		S	e		x		x		x		x		x	x			x			x		x			x	x	x	x	x	x		x		x		A	A			A	A	A		T
11.	**Leading— Influencing**																																															
11.01	Mathematics & Statistics		I		s	e	c		x		x		x	x			x	x		x		x		x			x	x	x	x		x		x		H	H	H	H		H				T/G
11.02	Educational & Library Services		i	a	S	e	c	x		x	x		x		x		x		x	x	x		x			x	x	x	x	x	x	x		x	x	H	H	A		A				T/G
11.03	Social Research	r	I	a	s	E	c	x		x	x		x	x		x	x	x		x		x			x	x	x	x		x	x	x		H	H	A		A				T/G
11.04	Law			a	S	e		x		x	x	x		x	x		x	x	x		x	x		x	x		x	x	x	x	x	x		H	H	H		A				C/G
11.05	Business Administration		i		s	E	c	x		x	x	x		x	x		x	x	x		x		x			x	x	x		x	x	x	x	H	H	A		A				T/G
11.06	Finance		i	a	s	E	c			x		x	x	x		x		x		x	x	x		x			x	x	x	x		x		H	H	H		A				T/G
11.07	Services Administration		i	a	S	e	c	x		x	x		x			x	x	x	x			x	x		x	x	x		x		x	x	H	H	A		A				T/G
11.08	Communications		i	A	s	e		x		x	x	x	x	x	x	x		x		x	x			x		x	x	x	x		x	x		H	H	A		A				C/G
11.09	Promotion			A	s	e		x		x	x		x		x		x	x	x		x		x	x			x	x		x	x		H	H	A		M	A		M	C/G
11.10	Regulations Enforcement		i		S	e	c	x		x	x	x		x	x			x	x		x		x	x	x	x		x	x	x	x	x	x	A	H	A	A	A	A	A		T/G
11.11	Business Management		i		s	E	c	x		x	x		x	x		x		x		x	x	x	x	x		x	x	x	x	x		x	x	A	H	A		A	A			T/G
11.12	Contracts & Claims	r			S	E	c	x		x	x		x	x	x	x		x		x	x		x			x	x		x	x		x		H	H	A		A				T/G
12.	**Physical Performing**																																															
12.01	Sports	r			S	e				x		x	x	x	x			x			x			x			x	x		x	x		x	x	A	A		A	A	A	H	H	H	H	O/G
12.02	Physical Feats	r			S	e				x			x	x			x			x			x			x	x		x	x		x	x	x	A			H	A		A	A	A	H	O/G

APPENDIX B
Bridges to Specific Careers

Chart 1   Relating Personal Characteristics to Selected Occupations

The following explains how to read the chart which appears on pages 106-11, which is adapted from Don Dillion, "Toward Matching Personal and Job Characteristics," *Occupational Outlook Quarterly*, 19, No. 1 (Spring 1975).

Column 1	Column 2	Column 3			4	5	6	7	8	9	10	11	12	13	14	15	16	17	18	19	20	21	22	23	24
	Occupational Interest Areas	DOT Code Numbers																							
00.	Worker Trait Group Subgroup #(.00) and Selected Occupation	Occupational Categories	Data, People, Things	Occupational Title	Occupational Themes	High-school Graduate	Comm. College or Tech. Training	College	Jobs Widely Scattered	Jobs Concentrated in Localities	Can See Physical Results of Work	Opportunity for Self-Expression	Works As Part of a Team	Works Independently	Work Is Closely Supervised	Directs Activities of Others	Generally Confined to Work Area	Overtime or Shift Work Required	Exposed to Weather Conditions	High Level of Responsibility	Requires Physical Stamina	Works with Details	Repetitious Work	Motivates Others	Competitive
00.00																									
WTG Number	(Personal Characteristics)																								

Column 1: WTG Number.   The U.S. Department of Labor has worked out two numerical classifications for job titles. One, the Worker Trait Group Number (WTG#) is reported in *The Guide for Occupational Exploration* which groups and numbers occupations on the basis of the personal characteristics of the employee.

When the double asterisk (**) appears in column 1, it refers you to Chart 2 of this appendix (pp. 112-15) where these double-asterisked occupations are related to Christian work environments. For example, many Christian outreach and support organizations employ writers and editors listed under 01.01.

Column 2: Occupational Interest Areas.   The twelve major occupational divisions from the GOE are listed. Within each of the twelve are groups of occupations that share the same set of worker traits. These *Worker Trait Group titles* appear opposite the four-digit number in column 1, for example, 01.01 Literary Arts. Finally, within each Worker Trait Group title are *Subgroup # (.00) and Selected Occupations*. For example, the first occupation under WTG 01.01 is ".01 Editor, Publications." Thus each occupation can be identified by a six-digit code. For "Editor, Publications" the code is "01.01.01."

Column 3: DOT Code Numbers.   The second classification by the U.S. Department of Labor is reported in the *Dictionary of Occupational Titles*. The DOT groups occupations according to the kinds of work performed. This nine-digit code has three parts: the first three digits indicate the occupational category, division and group; the second three indicate the worker skill levels —data skills, people skills and thing or manual skills (see p. 56); finally, the last three digits reflect the alphabetical order of occupations within an occupational grouping.

Column 4: Occupational Themes.   This is another system of coding occupations that is incorporated into the Strong-Campbell Interest Inventory. The system comes out of research of John L. Holland and is described in detail in *Making Vocational Choices: A Theory of Careers*. See page 52 for your code, based on the first letter of the three themes you chose. Your first place letter should appear as one of the three Occupational Themes assigned to occupations you consider. The greater the agreement between your code and the theme code the greater the potential for you to experience satisfaction in that occupation.

Column 5: High-school Graduate.   A high-school diploma is generally required.

Column 6: Community College or Technical Training.   Apprenticeship or some form of non-degree post-high-school training is required.

Column 7: College.   Requires at least a bachelor's degree. (C = B.A. or B.S. degree; G = graduate work or first professional degree.)

Column 8: Jobs Widely Scattered.   Jobs are located in most areas of the United States.

Column 9: Jobs Concentrated in Localities.   Jobs are highly concentrated in one or a few geographical locations.

Column 10: Can See Physical Results of Work.   Work produces a tangible product.

Column 11: Opportunity for Self-Expression.   Freedom to use one's own ideas.

Column 12: Works As Part of a Team.   Interacts with fellow employees in performing work.

Column 13: Works Independently.   Requires initiative, self-discipline and the ability to organize.

Column 14: Work Is Closely Supervised.   Job performance and work standards controlled by supervisor.

Column 15: Directs Activities of Others.   Work entails supervisory responsibilities.

Column 16: Generally Confined to Work Area.   Physically located at one work setting.

Column 17: Overtime or Shift Work Required.   Works hours other than normal daytime shifts; or completes the job regardless of time required.

Column 18: Exposed to Weather Conditions.   Works outside or is subjected to temperature extremes.

Column 19: High Level of Responsibility.   Requires making key decisions involving property, finances, or human safety and welfare.

Column 20: Requires Physical Stamina.   Must be in physical condition for continued lifting, standing and walking.

Column 21: Works with Details.   Works with technical data, numbers or written materials on a continuous basis.

Column 22: Repetitious Work.   Performs the same task on a continuing basis.

Column 23: Motivates Others.   Must be able to influence others.

Column 24: Competitive.   Competes with other people on the job for recognition and advancement, or with other businesses or organizations.

Column headers (rotated), columns 4–23:

- 4 = High-school Graduate
- 5 = Comm. College or Tech. Training
- 6 = College
- 7 = Jobs Widely Scattered
- 8 = Jobs Concentrated in Localities
- 9 = Can See Physical Results of Work
- 10 = Opportunity for Self-Expression
- 11 = Works As Part of a Team
- 12 = Works Independently
- 13 = Work Is Closely Supervised
- 14 = Directs Activities of Others
- 15 = Generally Confined to Work Area
- 16 = Overtime or Shift Work Required
- 17 = Exposed to Weather Conditions
- 18 = High Level of Responsibility
- 19 = Requires Physical Stamina
- 20 = Works with Details
- 21 = Repetitious Work
- 22 = Motivates Others
- 23 = Competitive

Column 1 = WTG Number **Column 2** = Occupational Interest Areas / Worker Trait Group Subgroup #(.00) and Selected Occupation (Personal Characteristics) **Column 3** = DOT Code Numbers (Occupational Categories Data, People, Things / Occupational Title) and Occupational Themes

Occupation	DOT Code	Themes	4	5	6	7	8	9	10	11	12	13	14	15	16	17	18	19	20	21	22	23
01. Artistic																						
01.01 Literary Arts																						
** .01 Editor, Publications	132.037-022	AIS			8*	x		x	x	x						x		x		x			x
** .02 Copy Writer	131.067-014	AIS			C	x		x	x							x		x		x			
** .02 Editorial Writer	131.067-022	AIS			C	x		x	x	x						x		x		x			
** .02 Writer	131.067-046	AIS			C	x			x	7*	x							x		x			
.03 Critic	131.067-018	AIS			8*	x			x							7*		x				x	x
01.01 Visual Arts																						
** .01 Teacher, Art	149.021-010	ASI			x			x				x	x	x				x		x		x	
** .02 Painter	144.061-010	ASI	3	7*	7*	x		x	x	x		x						x	x	x			7*
.03 Art Director	142.031-010	AIS			x		x	x	x	x			x					x		x		x	x
** .03 Audiovisual Production Specialist	149.061-010	ASI			x		x	x	x	x			x					x		x		x	x
** .03 Commercial Artist	141.061-022	AIS		x			x	x	x	x				x				x		x		x	
.03 Commercial Designer	141.081-014	AIS			C	x	x	x	x			x						x		x			x
** .03 Photojournalist	143.062-034	AIR			C	x		x	x			x				x	• x		x	x		x	x
01.03 Performing Arts: Drama																						
** .01 Dramatic Coach	150.027-010	ASE				x	x		x	x			x				x		x			x	x
** .01 Teacher, Drama	150.027-014	ASE			x			x				x	x				x		x			x	
** .02 Actors and Actresses	150.047-010	AIS		x				x			x						x					x	x
** .03 Radio and Television Announcer	159.147-010	EAR			3*	x			x					x		x						x	x
01.04 Performing Arts: Music																						
** .01 Choral Director	152.047-010	ASI			3*	x		x					x	x		x		x				x	
** .01 Teacher, Music	152.021-010	ASI			C	x		x				x	x	x		x		x				x	
** .03 Singer	152.047-022	AES			C	6*	x	x	x														x
** .04 Musician, Instrumental	152.041-010	ASI			C	6*	x	x	x							x							x
01.05 Performing Arts: Dance																						
.01 Choreographer	151.027-010	AES			x			x	x	x	x		x			x				x		x	x
01.06 Craft Arts																						
** .01 Photoengraver	971.381-022	AIR	x	x			x	x		x				x	x					x	x		
.02 Jeweler and Jewelry Repairer	700.281-010	RIS		x			x						x		x					x			
01.07 Elemental Arts																						
** .02 Announcer	159.347-010	EAR			3*	x		x	x					x	x	x						x	x
01.08 Modeling																						
.01 Instructor, Modeling	099.227-026	SRE		8*		x		x				x	x		x	x	x		x			x	x
.01 Model	297.667-014	ESC		x		x		x				x	x			x	7*		7*				x
02. Scientific																						
02.01 Physical Sciences																						
** .01 Astronomer	021.067-010	IAR			C		x	x		x													
** .01 Chemist	022.061-010	IRA			C	x		x		x													
** .01 Geographer	029.067-010	IRS			C	x		x		x										x			
** .01 Geologist	024.061-018	IRA			G		x	x		x										x			
** .01 Geophysicist	024.061-030	IRA			C		x	x		x										x			
** .01 Mathematician	020.067-014	IRA			C	x		x		x				x						x			
** .01 Meteorologist	025.062-010	IRA			C	x		x		x						x				x			
** .01 Physicist	023.061-014	IAR			C	x		x		x													
02.02 Life Sciences																						
.01 Biomedical Engineer	019.061-010	IRE			C		x	x	x	x			x							x			
** .02 Agronomist	040.061-010	IRS			3*	x		x	7*	7*			7*			x	x	x	x		7*		
.02 Range Manager	040.061-046	RIS			C	x				x						x		x					
** .02 Soil Conservationist	040.061-054	RIS			C	x				x						x				x			
** .02 Soil Scientist	040.061-058	RIS			C	x				x										x			
** .03 Biochemist	041.061-026	IRS			C	x		7*	x	7*			7*	7*			7*		x	7*		
** .03 Biologist	041.061-030	ISR			C	x		7*		7*				x		7*			x	7*		
** .04 Food Technologist	041.081-010	RIS			3*	x		x	x	7*			7*		7*	7*		7*	x	7*	7*	7*
02.03 Medical Sciences																						
** .01 General Practitioner	070.101-022	ISA			G	x		x	x				x			x		x		x			

*See notes at end of table.

**See Chart 2 (pp. 112-15).

Column 1	Column 2	Column 3	4	5	6	7	8	9	10	11	12	13	14	15	16	17	18	19	20	21	22	23	24
	** .01 Osteopathic Physician	071.101-010	ISR			G	x		x	x		x					x		x	7*	x		
	** .01 Physician, Occupational	070.101-078	ISA			G	x		x	x		x					x		x		x		
	.01 Podiatrist	079.101-022	SIR			G	x		x	x		x							x		x		
	** .02 Dentist	072.101-010	IRE			G	x		x	x		x					x		x		x		
	** .03 Veterinarian	073.101-010	RIS			G	x		x	x		x					x	x	x		x		
	.04 Chiropractor	079.101-010	ESR			3*	x		x	x		x					x		x	x	x		
	** .04 Optometrist	079.101-018	IRC			G	x		x	x		x					x		x		x		
	** .04 Speech Pathologist	076.107-010	ISA			G	x		x	x		x		x					x		x		
02.04	Laboratory Technology																						
	** .01 Chemical Laboratory Technician	022.261-010	IRA			3*	7*	7*	x			7*		x						x	7*		
	** .01 Laboratory Supervisor	022.137-010	IRA			3*	7*	7*		x	x			x					x		x		x
	** .01 Pharmacist	074.161-010	EIC			G	x				x					x		x		x		
	.02 Biological Aide	049.384-010	ISR		3*	7*	7*	7*	x		7*				x			x		x	7*	
	** .02 Medical-Laboratory Assistant	078.381-010	ISC	x	3*	7*	x	x			x		x			x		x		x		
03.	**Plants and Animals**																						
03.01	Managerial Work: Plants and Animals																						
	.01 Farmer, Cash Grain	401.161-101	RIC		3*	7*	x		x		x			x	x	x	x	x	x		7*	x	x
	** .01 Farmer, General	421.161-010	RCI		3*	7*	x		x		7*			7*	x	x	x	7*		7*		x
	** .03 Horticultural-Specialty Grower, Field	405.161-014	RIC			3*	x		x	x	x			x	x	x	x	x	x	x		x	x
	** .04 Forester	040.061-034	RIS			C	x					x		x		x	x	x	x			
03.02	General Supervision: Plants & Animals																						
	.03 Supervisor, Horticultural Specialty Farming	405.131-101	RIC		3*	7*	x		x		x			x			x	x	x		x	
	.03 Supervisor, Park Workers	406.134-014	RIC		3*	7*	x			x	x			x	x		x	x	7*		x	
03.03	Animal Training and Service																						
	.01 Animal Trainer	159.224-010	AES	8*			x		x	x				7*			7*	x	7*		7*	7*
	** .02 Animal Caretaker	410.674-010	RIC	x			x		x			7*					7*		7*			
03.04	Elemental Work: Plants and Animals																						
	.02 Forest Worker	452.687-010	RIC	x			x			x		x					x		x		x	
	.04 Greenskeeper 1	406.137-010	RIC	x			x			x		x					x		x		x	
04.	**Protective**																						
04.01	Safety and Law Enforcement																						
	.01 Police Chief	375.117-010	RES			3*		x		x		x		x		7*		x	x	x		x
	.02 FBI Special Agent	375.167-042	RES			G		x		x								x		x	x	x	
04.02	Security Services																						
	.01 Police Officer II	375.367-010	RES	x	7*		x					x	x				x	x	x	x	x	
	.03 Fire Fighter	373.364-010	RSE	x	7*		x		x		x		x	7*		7*	x	x	x		x	
05.	**Mechanical**																						
05.01	Engineering																						
	** .06 Industrial Engineer	012.167-030	RIE			3*	x		x	x				x				x		x		x
	.06 Mining Engineer	010.061-014	RIE			3*		x	x	x	x			x			x	x		x		7*
	.06 Production Engineer	012.167-046	IRE			G		x		x	x			x	x	7*		x		x		x	7*
	** .07 Aeronautical Engineer	002.061-014	IRE			3*		x	x	x	x			x				x		x		7*
	** .07 Architect	001.061-010	ARI		x	3*	x		x	x		x		x				x		x		7*	x
	** .07 Chemical Engineer	008.061-018	IRE			3*		x	x	x	x			x						x		7*
	** .07 Civil Engineer	005.061-014	RIE			3*	x		x	x	x			x				x		x		7*
	** .08 Agricultural Engineer	013.061-010	IRE			3*	x		x	x	x			x						x		7*
	** .08 Electronics Engineer	003.061-030	IRE			3*	x		x	x	x			x				7*		x		7*
	** .08 Mechanical Engineer	007.061-014	RIE			3*	x		x	x	x			x						x		7*
05.02	Managerial Work: Mechanical																						
	.03 Production Superintendent	183.117-014	ESC			8	x				x			x			7*	x		x		x
05.03	Engineering Technology																						
	** .01 Surveyor, Geodetic	018.167-038	RCI	x	2*	7*	x				x			x			x			x		
	** .02 Draftsman	017.161-010	RIE			3*	x				x		x		x					x		
	.02 Patternmaker	781.381-026	RCS	x	x		x			x		x		x		x				x		
	** .03 Air-Traffic-Control Specialist, Station	193.162-014	RIE		3*	7*			x	x				x	x			x		x	7*	
	** .06 Construction Inspector	182.267-010	ERI	x	x		x					x			x		x	x	x	x		
05.04	Air and Water Vehicle Operation																						
	** .01 Airplane Pilot	196.263-010	IRC			3*		x			x			x	x	x		x	x	x		
	.02 Pilot, Ship	197.133-026	REI			3*		x			x			x	x			x	x	x		
05.05	Craft Technology																						
	** .01 Bricklayer	861.381-014	RCS		x		x		x		x							x		x		
	** .02 Carpenter	860.381-022	RCI		x		x		x		x							x		x		
	** .03 Plumber	862.381-030	RIE		x		x		x		x		x							x		
	** .05 Electrician	824.261-010	RIS		x		x		x		x							x		x		
	** .05 Telephone Installer and Repairer	822.281-022	RIE	x			x				x						x	x		x	x	
	** .06 Sheet-Metal Worker	804.281-010	RIE	x	x		x		x		x						x			x		

Column 1 WTG Number	Column 2 Occupational Interest Areas / Worker Trait Group Subgroup #(.00) and Selected Occupation (Personal Characteristics)	Column 3 DOT Code Numbers / Occupational Title	4 Occupational Themes	5 High-school Graduate	6 Comm. College or Tech. Training	7 College	8 Jobs Widely Scattered	9 Jobs Concentrated in Localities	10 Can See Physical Results of Work	11 Opportunity for Self-Expression	12 Works As Part of a Team	13 Works Independently	14 Work Is Closely Supervised	15 Directs Activities of Others	16 Generally Confined to Work Area	17 Overtime or Shift Work Required	18 Exposed to Weather Conditions	19 High Level of Responsibility	20 Requires Physical Stamina	21 Works with Details	22 Repetitious Work	23 Motivates Others	24 Competitive
	** .07 Machine Repairer	600.280-042	RIE		x		x		x			x			7*					x	x	7*	
	.07 Tool-and-Die Maker	601.280-046	RIS		x		x	x	x			x	x		x	x				x	x		
	** .09 Automobile Mechanic	620.261-010	RIE		x		x		x			x			x				x				
	** .10 Instrument Repairer	722.281-010	IRC	x	x		x					x			x						x		
	.11 Optician	716.280-008	RIC	x	x		x					x									x		
	.12 Piano Tuner	730.361-010	RIC	x				x				x											
	** .13 Printing Press Operator & Assistant	651.362-010	RIC	x	x			x			x						x			x			
	.15 Shoe Repairer	365.361-014	RIC				x		x			x			x					x		x	
	** .17 Chef	313.131-014	RIS		x		x				x			x	x								
	** .17 Dietitian, Clinical	077.127-014	RIC			C	x					x		x						x			
05.06	Systems Operation																					
	** .01 Power Plant Operator	952.382-018	RIS		5		x		x		x		7*		x	x			x	x	x		
	** .02 Engineer	197.130-010	IRE	x	1*		x		x		x		7*		x		7*		x	x	x		
05.07	Quality Control-Mechanical																					
	** .02 Airplane Inspector	621.261-010	RIE		x		x								x	x	x	x		x	x		
	** .02 Auto-Repair-Service Estimator	620.261-018	RIE		2*		x		x			x		x	x					x			
05.08	Land/Water Vehicle Operation																					
	** .01 Truck Driver, Heavy	905.663-014	RCE	3*			x		x			x			x	x			x		x		
	.02 Locomotive Engineer	910.363-014	RES	x			x					x		x	x	x	x	x	x	x			
05.09	Materials Control																					
	** .01 Shipping and Receiving Clerk	222.387-050	RIC	1*			x				x		x		x				x		x		
	.01 Tool Crib Attendant	222.367-062	RIE	1*			x		x						x					x	x		
	.03 Meter Reader	209.567-010	RCS	1*			x		x							x	x		x	x	x		
05.10	Crafts: Mechanical																					
	.01 Roofer	866.381-010	RIE		x		x		x			x					x		x		7*		
	.02 Service Manager	185.167-058	ESC		x	7*	x			x				x	x		7*	x	7*	x		x	
	** .03 Appliance Repairer	723.584-010	RIC		x		x					x					x						
	** .07 Painter	840.381-010	RCI		x		x		x			x									x		
	.08 Meat Cutter	316.681-010	RSE		x		x					x			x						x		
05.11	Equipment Operation																					
	** .01 Operating Engineer	859.683-010	RIE	x	x		x		x			x					x		x	x			
	.03 Rotary Driller	930.382-026	RIC		5*		x		x		x			x		x	7*		x	x			
	.04 Crane II Operator	921.663-022	RCS		5*		x		x		x			x			x		x				
05.12	Elemental Work: Mechanical																					
	.05 Brake Coupler, Road Freight	910.367-010	RES	7*			x					x					x	x	x	x	x		
	** .18 Hotel Housekeeper and Assistant	321.137-010	SRE	7*			x						x		x						x		
06.	**Industrial**																					
06.01	Production Technology																					
	04. Molder	518.361-010	RSE		x		x		x		x		x		x						x		
	.04 Watch Repairer	715.281-010	RIE		x		x		x		x	x			x						x		
06.02	Production Work																					
	.01 Supervisor	500.131-010	RIE	3*			x					x		x						x	7*	7*	
	.22 Assembler	706.361-010	RIC	3*			x					x				x			7*	7*	x		
	.27 Garment Cutter	781.584-014	RCS	1*				x	x				x		x				x		x		
06.03	Quality Control-Industrial																					
	** .01 Inspector 1	619.364-010	RIC	3*	7*		x		x			x	x		x		7*		7*	x		
	.02 Grader	669.587-010	RIC	3*	7*		x		x						x				7*	x	x		
	.02 Lumber Inspector	669.587-010	RCE	1*				x	x						x	7*	7*		x	x	x		
06.04	Elemental Work: Industrial																					
	** .01 Packaging Supervisor	920.132-010	RES	x			x		x			x		x	x				7*		x	7*	7*
	.11 Chemical Operator 2	558.585-014	RCS		x	7*	x		x				x	x	x				7*	x	x		
	.27 Dressmaker	785.361-010	RCS		5*		x		x	7*					7*			x		x			
	.38 Crater	920.484-010	RES	1*			x		x						x	7*	7*		x				
07.	**Business Detail**																					
07.01	Administrative Detail																					
	.01 Loan Counselor	186.267-014	SEA			3*	x		x			x			x			7*		x			

Column 1	Column 2	Column 3	4	5	6	7	8	9	10	11	12	13	14	15	16	17	18	19	20	21	22	23	24
	**.02 Manager, Office	169.167-034	ESC			x	7*	x			x				x		7*		7*		x	7*	7*	
	.02 Station Agent 1	910.137-038	RES		7*			x				x			x	x	x					x		
	**.02 Teacher Aide	099.321-010	SAE		5*			x			7*	x		x		x								x	
	**.03 Medical Secretary	201.362-014	CSA		5*			x					7*			x				7*		x			
	**.05 Hospital-Insurance Representative	166.267-014	SEC				C	x					x									x	7*		
07.02	Mathematical Detail																							
	**.01 Bookkeeper (Clerical) 1	210.382-014	CSI			x		x			x		x			x						x	x		
	**.02 Account Analyst	214.382-010	CIS			x		x			x		x			x						x	x		
	.03 Claim Examiner	168.267-014	SIE			x		x			x		x			x						x	x		
	.03 Statistical Clerk	216.382-062	CIS	x				x				x		x		x						x	x		
07.03	Financial Detail																							
	**.01 Cashier 1	211.362-010	CSI		1*			x					x	x		x						x	x		
	.01 Cashier 2	211.462-010	CSI		1*			x					x	x		x						x	x		
	.01 Post-Office Clerk	243.367-014	CES	x				x				x				x	x			x	x				
07.04	Oral Communications																							
	**.02 Foreign-Trade-Services Clerk	209.262-010	CIS		8*			x		x		7*				7*				7*		x			
	.03 Hotel Clerk	238.362-010	ESC	x				x				x				x	x					x			
	**.03 Reservations Agent	238.367-018	CSR	1*				x		x						x	7*					x			
	**.04 Receptionist	237.367-038	CSE	x				x				x				x						x			
07.05	Records Processing																							
	**.01 Traffic Clerk	221.367-078	CES	x				x	x			x				x	x								
	**.03 Medical-Record Clerk	245.362-010	CES				C	x				x										x	x		
	**.03 Medical-Record Technician	079.367-014	SIR				C	x				x										x	x		
	**.03 Stenographer	202.362-014	CES	x				x		x		x	x		x							x	x		
07.06	Clerical Machine Operation																							
	**.01 Computer Operator	213.362-010	CES	x				x				x		x		x	x					x	x		
	**.02 Typist	203.582-066	CIE	x				x		x			x	x		x						x	x		
	.02 Biller	214.482-010	CRI	x				x		x			x	x		x						x	x		
07.07	Clerical Handling																							
	**.01 File Clerk 1	206.362-010	CRS	x				x				x		x								x	x		
	.03 Clerk, General	209.562-010	CES	x				x				x		x		x						x	x		
08.	**Selling**																							
08.01	Sales Technology																							
	.01 Pharmaceutical Detailer	262.157-010	SER				C	x			x		x				7*	7*	x		x			x	x
	.01 Sales Representative, Dental & Medical Equipment	276.257-010	SER				C	x			x		x				7*	7*	x	7*	x			x	x
	.02 Sales Agent, Financial Services	251.257-010	ECS				3*	x			x		x				7*	7*	x		x			x	x
	**.03 Business-Opportunity and Property-Investment Broker	189.157-010	ESC				3*	x			x		x				x	7*	x		x			x	x
	**.03 Buyer	162.157-018	ECS				3*	x			x		x				x	7*	x		x			x	x
08.02	General Sales	(Search 250.0																						
	(Choose your preference in sales)	to 299.6)	ES9*				3*	x			x	7*	7*						7*	7*	x			x
	**.01 Manufacturer's Representative	279.157-010	ESI			x	3*	x			x		x				x	x		7*	x		x	x
08.03	Vending																							
	**.01 Photographer	143.457-010	AIE	x		x		x		x	x		x								x			x
	.01 Sales, Door-to-Door	291.457-018	ESC	3*				x		7*	x	7*	7*		7*				7*	7*	7*	x			x
09.	**Accommodating**																							
09.01	Hospitality Services																							
	**.01 Counselor, Camp	159.124-010	SEA				3*	x			x	x				x		x	x	x	x			x
	.03 Host/Hostess, Restaurant	310.137-010	SEC	1*				x		x			x			7*	x	7*		7*	x			
	.04 Airplane-Flight Attendant	352.367-010	ESA	x					x			x					x			x				
09.02	Barber and Beauty Services																							
	.01 Cosmetologist	332.271-010	SAC			x		x		x						x								
	.02 Barber	330.371-010	RSE			x		x		x						x						x		
09.03	Passenger Services																							
	**.01 Bus Driver	913.463-010	RCS		5*			x			x					x	7*		x	x	x			
	.02 Chauffeur	913.663-010	RSE	4*				x						x		x		x			x			
	**.03 Instructor, Driving	099.223-010	SRE				x					x		x		7*	x	x		x	x		
09.04	Customer Services																							
	.01 Waiter-Waitress, Informal	311.477-026	RSE	1*				x			x					x			x					
	**.02 Manager, Branch Store	369.467-010	SRE	8*		8*		x		x		x			7*	x				x			
09.05	Attendant Services																							
	**.02 Cafeteria Attendant	311.677-010	RSE	1*				x				x				x			x					
	.03 Bell Captain	324.137-014	SCE	1*				x				x				x			x					
10.	**Humanitarian**																							
10.01	Social Services																							

Column 1 / Column 2 — Occupational Interest Areas, Worker Trait Group, Subgroup #(.00) and Selected Occupation (WTG Number / Personal Characteristics)	Column 3 — DOT Code Numbers	4 Occupational Themes	5 High-school Graduate	6 Comm. College or Tech. Training	7 College	8 Jobs Widely Scattered	9 Jobs Concentrated in Localities	10 Can See Physical Results of Work	11 Opportunity for Self-Expression	12 Works As Part of a Team	13 Works Independently	14 Work Is Closely Supervised	15 Directs Activities of Others	16 Generally Confined to Work Area	17 Overtime or Shift Work Required	18 Exposed to Weather Conditions	19 High Level of Responsibility	20 Requires Physical Stamina	21 Works with Details	22 Repetitious Work	23 Motivates Others	24 Competitive
**.01 Clergy Member/Chaplain	120.007-010	SAI			G	x					x		x								x	
**.01 Director of Religious Activities	129.107-018	SAI			3*	x				x			x		x		x				x	
.02 Caseworker	195.107-010	SIA			G	x			7*	7*			7*				x				x	
**.02 Counselor	045.107-010	SEA			G	x			7*	7*			7*				x				x	
**.02 Psychologist, Clinical	045.107-022	IAS			G	x			x	7*			x				x			x	x	
**.02 Psychologist, Counseling	045.107-026	IAS			G	x			7*	x			7*		7*		x			7*	x	
**.02 Psychologist, School	045.107-034	IAS			G	x			x				x	x			x			x	x	
**.02 Social Worker, Delinquency Prevention	195.107-026	SIA			3*	x			7*	x			x				x				x	
**.02 Vocational-Rehabilitation Counselor	045.107-042	SIA			G	x				x			x				x				x	
10.02 Nursing, Therapy & Specialized Teaching Services																						
**.01 Nurse, General Duty	075.374-010	SIA		4*	4*	x				x		x	7*				x		x	x		
**.01 Nurse, Head	075.127-018	SIA		4*	4*	x				x		x	x				x		x	x		
**.01 Nurse, Licensed Practical	079.374-014	CRI		5*		x				x		x					x		x	x		
.02 Art Therapist	076.127-010	ASI			3*	x			x	7*	x		x	x	7*		x				x	
.02 Dental Hygienist	078.361-010	IRS	x			x					x		x							x		
.02 Music Therapist	076.127-014	SIR			3*	x			x	7*	x		x	x	7*		x				x	
**.02 Occupational Therapist	076.121-010	RIA			C	x		x	x	x			x				x		x			
**.02 Physical Therapist	076.121-014	IRS			4*	x		x	x	x			x				x				x	
**.02 Physical Therapist Assistant	076.224-010	SIR		5*		x		x	x	x		x										
**.02 Radiologic Technologist	078.362-026	RIS			C	x				x		x		x			x		x			
.02 Recreational Therapist	076.124-014	SIR			3*	x		x	x	x	7*		x			7*	x		x		x	
**.03 Teacher, Handicapped Students	094.227-018	SAI			3*	x			x	7*	x		x	x	7*		x				x	
10.03 Child and Adult Care																						
.01 Electroencephalograph Technician	078.362-022	ISR	x			x				x		x							x	x		
**.02 Medical Assistant	079.367-010	SIR	x			x				x		x							x			
**.03 Attendant, Children's Institution	359.677-010	SRE		3*		x		x		x		x	x		7*							
.03 Companion	309.677-010	RSE	1*			x				x		x			x	x						
11. Leading—Influencing																						
11.01 Mathematics and Statistics																						
**.01 Statistician, Mathematical	020.067-022	IAS			C	x			x	x			x				x					
**.01 Systems Analyst, Electronic Data Processing	012.167-066	ESI			C	x	x		x				7*				x					
**.02 Actuary	020.167-010	IEC			C		x		x	x			x				x		x			
.02 Consultant	189.167-010	ESC			4*	x			x	7*	x		7*		x		x		x		x	x
**.02 Financial Analyst	020.167-014	CEI			G	x			x	7*	x				7*		x		x		x	x
11.02 Educational and Library Services																						
**.01 Faculty Member, College or Univ.	090.227-010	IAS			G	x			x		x		x				x					
**.01 Teacher, Elementary School	092.227-010	SCA			C	x			x		x		x		x		x			x	x	
**.01 Teacher, Secondary School	091.227-010	SAE			C	x			x		x		x		x		x				x	
**03 Home Economist	096.121-014	SAE			C	x			x		x		x								x	
**.04 Career-Guidance Technician	249.367-014	CSA		4*	4*	x				x		x							x		7*	
**.04 Librarian	100.127-014	SAI			G	x				x							x		x			
**.04 Library Technician	100.167-018	SAI	x			x				x							x		x			
**.04 Media Specialist, School Library	100.167-030	SAI		4*	4*	x	x			x					7*			7*	x	7*		
11.03 Social Research																						
**.01 Psychologist, Developmental	045.061-010	ISA			G	x		x	x	x	7*		7*						x			
**.01 Psychologist, Educational	045.067-010	ISA			G	x			x	x	x		x						x		x	
.01 Psychologist, Experimental	045.061-018	ISA			G	x		x	x	x	7*		x						x			
.01 Psychologist, Industrial-Organizational	045.107-030	ISA			G	x			x	x	7*		x						x		x	
**.02 Political Scientist	051.067-010	SIA			C	x			x	x	x								x			
**.02 Sociologist	054.067-014	SIA			G	x			x	x	x								x			
**.02 Urban Planner	199.167-014	IRA			G		x		x	x			x				x		x		x	
**.02 Scientific Linguist	059.067-014	ISA			G	x			x	7*			7*				x		x			
**.03 Anthropologist	055.067-010	IAR			G	x			x	x			x						x			
**.03 Historian	052.067-022	SEI			G	x			x	x	x								x			
.04 Job Analyst	166.267-018	SEC			4*	x			x	7*			x			7*	x		x		x	
**.05 Economist	050.067-010	ECI			G	x			x		x		x						x			

Column 1	Column 2	Column 3	4	5	6	7	8	9	10	11	12	13	14	15	16	17	18	19	20	21	22	23	24
11.04	Law																						
**.01	Judge	111.107-010	ESA			G	x			x		x						x		x			
**.02	Lawyer	110.107-010	ESA			G	x			x		x				x		x		x		7*	x	x
**.02	Paralegal Assistant	119.267-026	ESA			4*	x					x	x		x						x	7*		
11.05	Business Administration																						
**.01	Association Executive	189.117-010	ESC			4*	x			x	x			x		x		x		x		x	x
**.01	President (any industry)	189.117-026	ECI			G	x							x				x		x		x	x
**.02	Administrative Assistant	169.167-010	ESC			C	x			x		x		7*	x			x					
.02	Manager, Branch	183.117-010	ESC			G	x			x	x			x				x		x		x	
**.02	Manager, Operations	184.117-050	ESC			4*	x				x			x			7*	x		x		x	
**.02	Manager, Personnel	166.117-018	ESC			4*	x			x	x			x				x		x		x	
.03	Manager, City	188.117-114	ESC			G	x			7*	x			x		7*		x		x			
**.04	Purchasing Agent	162.157-038	ERC			C	x					x		x				x		x		x	x
11.06	Finance																						
**.01	Accountant	160.167-010	CES			C	x					x			x						x	x		
.03	Credit Officer, Dealer Accounts	161.267-014	CES			C	x					x						x		x	x		
.03	Market-Research Analyst 1	050.067-014	IAS			G	x					x	x					x		x			x
.03	Underwriter	169.167-058	ECS			C	x		x			x						x		x			
.04	Stockbroker	251.157-010	ESA			C	x		x		7*				x	7*	x		x		x	x
11.07	Services Administration																						
**.01	Administrator, Social Welfare	195.117-010	SEC			G	x					x		x		x		x		x		
**.03	Principal	099.117-018	SIE			G	x			x	x			x		x		x		x		
**.03	College President	190.117-034	SEI			G	x							x				x		x		
.04	Superintendent, Recreation	187.117-054	SEA			C	x		x	7*	7*					x		7*	x	x			x	7*
11.08	Communications																						
**.01	Editor	132.037-014	AIS		8*	G	x			x	x			x			7*		x			
**.02	Reporter	131.267-018	ASE			C	x		x	x	x			x	7*		x		x	x	x			x
**.02	Writer, Technical Publications	131.267-026	ASI			4*	x			x	7*	x		7*					x			
**.03	Newscaster	131.267-010	AIS			4*	x			x	x							x		x		
11.09	Promotion																						
**.01	Manager, Advertising	163.167-010	AES			C	x			x	x			x				x		x		x	
.01	Account Executive	164.167-010	AES			8*	x			x	7*			7*				x		x		x	x
.01	Fashion Coordinator	185.157-010	ESA			8*	x		x	x	x			x				x				x	x
**.03	Public Relations Representative	165.067-010	AES			C		x		x	x					x				x		x	x
11.10	Regulations Enforcement																						
.01	Investigator	168.267-062	SIE			3*	x				7*	x				7*				x			
**.02	Equal-Opportunity Representative	168.167-014	ESI			G	x			x	7*			7*				x		x		x	
**.03	Health Officer, Field	168.167-018	SIE			G	x				x			x				x			
.03	Safety Inspector	168.167-078	SIE			3*	x				7*	x				7*		7*	x			
.03	Food and Drug Inspector	168.267-042	SIC			C	x		x		7*							x		x		7*
11.11	Business Management																						
**.01	Manager, Apartment House	186.167-046	ESC		8*	4*	x					x		x		x		x		x		
.04	Manager, Insurance Agency	186.167-034	ESC			C	x							x		x		x		x		x	x
.04	Manager, Restaurant	187.167-106	ESC			C	x		x		x			x	x			x			
.05	Manager, Retail Store	185.167-046	ESE			C	x				x			x		x		x		x		x	x
11.12	Contracts and Claims																						
.01	Claim Adjuster	241.217-010	SER	x			x					x				x			x			
.01	Claim Examiner	241.267-018	SER	x			x					x		x			x			x	x		
.01	Manager, Customer Service	168.167-058	ESC		8*	C	x					x		x				x		x		
.02	Real-Estate Agent	186.117-058	ESC	8*		4*	x					x				x		x		x		x	x
12.	**Physical Performing**																						
12.01	Sports																						
**.01	Head Coach	153.117-010	SRE			G	x			x	x			x				x		x	x	x		x
.03	Professional Athlete	153.341-010	SRE	4*	4*	4*	x		x	x	7*	7*					x			x		x		x
12.02	Physical Feats																						
.01	Stunt Performer	159.341-014	SRE	4*	4*	4*				x	7*	7*									7*		x

*Notes

1. Requirements vary according to the type of industry.
2. Postsecondary schooling required, usually in community college, technical or vocational school.
3. Educational requirements vary according to area of work. For details do a field survey and/or see: *The Guide for Occupational Exploration, The Occupational Outlook Handbook* and *The Dictionary of Occupational Titles.*
4. Type of training program depends on individual preference.
5. Training programs are available from vocational schools or community colleges.
6. Teachers only.
7. May at times include this characteristic.
8. Requires education plus experience.
9. ES?; the third characteristic should reflect an area of your education or training: R, I, A, or C. See Appendix A.

**See Chart 2 (pp. 112-15).

Chart 2. Relating Selected Occupations to Christian Work Environments (Note: See appendix D, part II for additional sources of information.)

Occupations by WTG	Bookstores	Camps	Children's Homes/Family Service Agencies	Church and Mission—Central Administration	Disaster Relief	Drug/Alcohol Rehabilitation	Films/Recordings/Radio/TV	Local Church	Mass Evangelism/Conferences	Mission—Action Programs	Mission—Aviation Services	Mission—Bible Translation	Mission—Hospital/Clinic	Publishers	Retirement/Convalescent Homes	Schools—Day School/Bible Inst./College
01.01																
.01 Editor				×			×		×	×		×		×		×
.02 Copy Writer				×			×		×	×				×		×
.02 Editorial Writer				×			×		×	×		×				×
.02 Writer				×			×		×	×				×		×
01.02																
.01 Art Teacher		×														×
.02 Painter		×		×			×			×				×		×
.03 Audiovisual Production				×			×		×	×		×		×		×
.03 Commercial Artist				×			×		×	×		×		×		×
.03 Photojournalist							×		×	×						×
01.03																
.01 Drama Coach							×									×
.01 Teacher, Drama							×									×
.02 Actors/Actresses				×			×		×	×						×
.03 Radio/TV Announcer							×									×
01.04																
.01 Choral Director		×						×								×
.01 Teacher, Music		×						×								×
.03 Singer							×	×	×							×
.04 Musician, Instrumental							×	×	×							×
01.06																
.01 Photoengraver														×		
01.07																
.02 Announcer							×		×							
02.01																
.01 Astronomer																×
.01 Chemist																×
.01 Geographer																×
.01 Geophysicist																×
.01 Mathematician																×
.01 Meteorologist																×
.01 Physicist																×
02.02																
.02 Agronomist				×						×						×
.02 Soil Conservationist				×						×						×
.02 Soil Scientist				×						×						×
.03 Biochemist													×			×
.03 Biologist						×				×			×			×
.04 Food Technologist		×	×							×						×
02.03																
.01 General Practitioner					×	×				×			×			×
.01 Osteopathic Physician					×	×				×			×			×
.01 Physician					×	×				×			×			×
.02 Dentist										×			×			×
.03 Veterinarian		×								×						×
.04 Optometrist										×					×	×
.04 Speech Pathologist										×						×
02.04																
.01 Chemical Lab Technician													×			×
.01 Laboratory Supervisor													×			×

Column list (upper section):

.02 Engineer

05.07
.02 Airplane Inspector
.02 Auto-Repair Estimator

05.08
.01 Truck Driver, Heavy

05.09
.01 Shipping/Receiving Clerk

05.10
.03 Appliance Repairer
.07 Painter

05.11
.01 Operating Engineer

05.12
.18 Hotel Housekeeper/Asst.

06.03
.01 Inspector

06.04
.01 Packaging Supervisor

07.01
.02 Manager, Office
.02 Teacher Aide
.03 Medical Secretary
.05 Hospital Insurance Rep.

07.02
.01 Bookkeeper (Clerical)
.02 Account Analyst

07.03
.01 Cashier

Column list (lower section):

.01 Pharmacist
.02 Medical Lab Assistant

03.01
.01 Farmer
.03 Horticultural Grower
.04 Forester

03.03
.02 Animal Caretaker

05.01
.06 Industrial Engineer
.07 Aeronautical Engineer
.07 Architect
.07 Chemical Engineer
.07 Civil Engineer
.08 Agricultural Engineer
.08 Electronics Engineer
.08 Mechanical Engineer

05.03
.01 Surveyor, Geodetic
.02 Draftsman
.03 Air-Traffic Controller
.06 Construction Inspector

05.04
.01 Airplane Pilot

05.05
.01 Bricklayer
.02 Carpenter
.03 Plumber
.05 Electrician
.05 Telephone Installer
.06 Sheet-Metal Worker
.07 Machine Repairer
.09 Automobile Mechanic
.10 Instrument Repairer
.13 Printer
.17 Chef
.17 Dietitian, Clinical

05.06
.01 Power Plant Operator

Occupations by WTG — Groups 09 and 10

Occupations by WTG	Bookstores	Camps	Children's Homes/Family Service Agencies	Church and Mission—Central Administration	Disaster Relief	Drug/Alcohol Rehabilitation	Films/Recordings/Radio/TV	Local Church	Mass Evangelism/Conferences	Mission—Action Programs	Mission—Aviation Services	Mission—Bible Translation	Mission—Hospital/Clinic	Publishers	Retirement/Convalescent Homes	Schools—Day School/Bible Inst./College
09.01																
.01 Counselor, Camp		×	×	×		×			×	×						
09.03																
.01 Bus Driver		×	×			×		×	×	×	×		×		×	×
.03 Instructor, Driving																×
09.04																
.02 Manager, Branch Store	×	×			×		×									×
09.05																
.02 Cafeteria Attendant		×	×	×		×				×					×	×
10.01																
.01 Clergy Member/Chaplain		×	×	×		×	×	×	×	×			×		×	×
.01 Dir. of Religious Activities		×	×	×	×	×	×	×	×	×			×		×	×
.02 Counselor		×	×		×	×	×	×	×	×		×	×		×	×
.02 Psychologist, Clinical						×						×	×			×
.02 Psychologist, Counseling		×	×	×	×	×	×	×	×	×			×		×	×
.02 Psychologist, School		×	×	×	×	×	×	×	×	×			×			×
.02 Social Worker, Delinquency Prevention			×			×										
.02 Vocational-Rehabilitation Counselor		×	×	×	×	×	×	×	×	×			×		×	×
10.02																
.01 Nurse, General Duty		×	×		×	×				×			×		×	×
.01 Nurse, Head		×	×		×	×				×			×		×	×
.01 Nurse, Licensed Practical			×		×	×				×			×		×	×
.02 Occupational Therapist						×				×			×		×	×

Occupations by WTG — Groups 07 and 08

Occupations by WTG	Bookstores	Camps	Children's Homes/Family Service Agencies	Church and Mission—Central Administration	Disaster Relief	Drug/Alcohol Rehabilitation	Films/Recordings/Radio/TV	Local Church	Mass Evangelism/Conferences	Mission—Action Programs	Mission—Aviation Services	Mission—Bible Translation	Mission—Hospital/Clinic	Publishers	Retirement/Convalescent Homes	Schools—Day School/Bible Inst./College
07.04																
.02 Foreign-Trade-Services Clerk				×			×	×	×	×	×					
.03 Reservations Agent			×							×			×			×
.04 Receptionist								×	×	×				×		
07.05																
.01 Traffic Clerk				×						×			×			×
.03 Medical-Record Clerk						×				×			×		×	×
.03 Medical-Record Technician						×				×			×		×	×
.03 Stenographer	×	×	×	×	×	×	×	×	×	×	×	×	×	×	×	×
07.06																
.01 Computer Operator	×	×	×	×	×		×		×	×		×	×	×		×
.02 Typist	×	×	×	×	×	×	×	×	×	×	×	×	×	×	×	×
07.07																
.01 File Clerk	×	×	×	×	×	×	×	×	×	×	×	×	×	×	×	×
08.01																
.03 Business Investment Broker	×			×												
.03 Buyer				×	×					×			×	×		×
08.02																
.01 Sales Representative	×	×			×		×		×					×		×
08.03																
.01 Photographer				×			×		×	×				×		×

.02 Physical Therapist										x			x		x	x
.02 Physical Therapist Asst.										x			x		x	
.02 Radiologic Technologist													x			
.03 Teacher for Handicapped						x				x					x	x
10.03																
.02 Medical Assistant		x	x		x	x				x			x		x	x
.03 Attendant, Children's Institution		x	x						x	x		x	x			x
11.01																
.01 Statistician, Math				x												x
.01 Systems Analyst				x	x		x		x	x		x	x	x		x
.02 Actuary				x	x					x						x
.02 Financial Analyst	x			x			x			x			x	x		x
11.02																
.01 Faculty Member, College	x	x	x	x		x	x		x	x		x		x		x
.01 Teacher, Elementary	x	x	x	x		x		x	x	x		x				x
.01 Teacher, Secondary	x	x	x	x		x		x	x	x		x				x
.03 Home Economist		x	x		x	x				x			x		x	x
.04 Career-Guidance Technician		x	x			x	x		x	x						x
.04 Librarian	x			x			x	x		x		x	x	x		x
.04 Library Technician	x			x			x	x		x		x	x	x		x
.04 Media Specialist				x			x	x	x	x		x		x		x
11.03																
.01 Psychologist, Developmental		x	x			x	x			x					x	x
.01 Psychologist, Educational		x	x				x		x	x		x				x
.02 Political Scientist					x				x	x						x
.02 Scientific Linguist				x						x		x				x
.02 Sociologist			x		x	x			x	x					x	x
.02 Urban Planner				x	x				x	x						x
.03 Anthropologist				x	x					x		x				x
.03 Historian				x			x			x						x
.05 Economist				x	x					x				x		x
11.04																
.02 Lawyer			x	x						x						x
.02 Paralegal Assistant			x	x	x	x				x			x			x
11.05																
.01 Association Executive	x	x	x	x	x	x	x		x	x	x	x	x	x	x	x
.01 Chief Executive (President)	x	x	x	x	x	x	x		x	x	x	x	x	x	x	
.02 Administrative Assistant	x		x		x		x		x	x		x	x	x	x	x
.02 Manager, Operations	x	x			x				x	x			x		x	
.02 Manager, Personnel	x	x	x	x	x	x	x		x	x	x	x	x	x	x	x
.04 Purchasing Agent	x	x	x	x	x		x			x			x	x	x	x

11.06																
.01 Accountant	x			x			x		x	x		x	x	x		x
11.07																
.01 Administrator, Social Welfare		x	x		x	x				x			x			
.03 Principal																x
.03 College President																x
11.08																
.01 Editor				x			x			x		x		x		
.02 Reporter				x			x			x						
.02 Writer, Technical Publications					x		x			x		x		x		x
.03 Newscaster							x									
11.09																
.01 Manager, Advertising	x	x		x	x		x		x	x				x		x
.03 Public Relations Representative		x	x	x	x	x	x		x	x				x		x
11.10																
.02 Equal-Opportunity Representative			x		x	x				x						x
.03 Health Officer, Field					x					x		x				x
11.11																
.01 Manager, Apartment House		x	x		x				x	x			x		x	x
12.01																
.01 Head Coach		x	x			x				x						x

APPENDIX C
Resources for Exploration of Career Options

The Academy Catalog. Chicago, Ill.: International Academy of Merchandising and Design, Limited, 1978.

Allied Health Education Programs in Junior and Senior Colleges. Hyattsville, Md.: U.S. Department of Health, Education, and Welfare, 1975.

Allied Medical Education Directory. 8th ed. Chicago, Ill.: American Medical Association, 1979.

Bestor, Dorothy D. *Aside from Teaching English What in the World Can You Do?* Seattle, Wash.: Univ. of Washington Press, 1977.

Business Economics Careers. Cleveland, Ohio: National Association of Business Economics, 1975 (pamphlet).

Campus Life's Guide to Christian Colleges. Wheaton, Ill.: Youth for Christ, 1981.

Career Index. Moravia, N.Y.: Chronicle Guidance Publications, Inc., 1976.

A Career in Science: Is It for You? A Guide for Handicapped Students. Irvine, Calif.: University of California, Career Planning and Placement Center and the School of Biological Sciences, 1978.

Career Information for College Graduates. Bethlehem, Pa.: College Placement Council, Inc., 1976.

Career Opportunities: Community Service and Related Specialists. New York: Doubleday, 1975.

Catalyst–Career Options Series for Undergraduate Women. New York: Catalyst, 1976, (Series of twelve booklets):
"Launching Your Career."
"Planning for Career Options."
"Have You Considered Government and Politics?"
"Have You Considered Industrial Management?"
"Have You Considered Finance?"
"Have You Considered Engineering?"
"Have You Considered Retail Management?"
"Have You Considered Accounting?"
"Have You Considered Sales?"
"Have You Considered Restaurant Management?"
"Have You Considered Insurance?"
"Have You Considered Banking?"

Claxton, Ronald H. and Biddie Lorenzen. *The Student Guide to Mass Media Internships.* Boulder, Co.: Intern Research Group, School of Journalism, Univ. of Colorado, 1979.

The College Handbook. New York: College Entrance Examination Board, 1975.

College Placement Annual. Bethlehem, Pa.: College Placement Council, Inc., 1981.

Dictionary of Occupational Titles. 4th ed. Washington, D.C.: Superintendent of Documents, U.S. Government Printing Office, 1977.

Education Directory: Colleges and Universities. Washington D.C.: U.S. Department of Health, Education, and Welfare, 1975.

Federal Career Directory. Washington, D.C.: Superintendent of Documents, U.S. Government Printing Office, 1976.

Guide to Federal Career Literature. Washington, D.C.: Superintendent of Documents, U.S. Government Printing Office, 1974.

Handbook of Trade and Technical Careers and Training. Washington, D.C.: National Association of Trade and Technical Schools.

Health Careers Planning Guide. Urbana, Ill.: Univ. of Illinois, 1976.

Johnson, Willis L., ed. *Directory of Special Programs for Minority Group Members: Career Information Services, Employment Skills Banks, Financial Aid Sources,* 2nd ed., Garrett Park, Md.: 1975.

Livesey, Herbert B. and Harold Doughty. *Guide to American Graduate Schools.* New York: Penguin, 1977.

McKee, Bill. *New Careers for Teachers.* Chicago, Ill.: Henry Regnery Co., 1972.

Malnig, Lawrence R. and Sandra L. Morrow. *What Can I Do with a Major in . . . ?* Jersey City, N.J.: Saint Peter's College Press, 1975.

Manual of Training for Business and Industry. Scranton, Pa.: Intext, Inc., 1975.·

Mitchell, Joyce Slayton. *I Can Be Anything: Careers and Colleges for Young Women.* New York: College Entrance Examination Board, 1978.

A Newspaper Career and You. Princeton, N.J.: Newspaper Fund, 1976.

Newspaper Internships for College Students. Princeton, N.J.: The Newspaper Fund, Inc., 1978.

Occupational Outlook Handbook. 1976-77 edition. Washington, D.C.: Superintendent of Documents, U.S. Government Printing Office, 1976-77.

Prelaw Handbook. Washington, D.C.: Association of American Law Schools and the Law School Admission Council, (current year).

Schola, Nelle Tumlin, et. al. *How to Decide: A Guide for Women.* New York: College Entrance Examination Board, 1975.

Shingleton, John D. and Phil Frank. *Which Niche?* East Lansing, Mich.: John D. Shingleton and Phil Frank, 1969.

Taking Care of Business: Exploring Career Possibilities in Business (Highlights from a Forum for Undergraduate Black Students). Atlanta, Ga.: 1977.

Teal, Everett A. *The Occupational Thesaurus,* vols. 1 and 2. Bethlehem, Pa.: Lehigh Univ., 1971.

Thain, Richard J. *The Managers: Career Alternatives for the College Educated.* The College Placement Council, Inc., 1978.

Walker, John H. III. *Thinking about Graduate School: A Planning Guide for Freshman and Sophomore Minority College Students.* Princeton, N.J.: Educational Testing Service, 1974.

Westbrook, Bert W. *Career Development Needs of Adults.* Washington, D.C.: American Personnel and Guidance Association and The National Vocational Guidance Association, 1978.

Wiggs, Garland, ed. *Career Opportunities: Marketing, Business and Office Specialists.* New York: Doubleday, 1975.

APPENDIX D
Resources for Identifying Prospective Employers

Note: Directories—listings of organizations and executives.

Information—write for advice on how to obtain additional directory information and possible job vacancies.

I. *Business and Industry*
Directories:

The Becker Guide. Chicago, Ill.: Becker and Warburg-Paribas Group, Inc., 1975.

College Placement Annual 1978. Bethlehem, Pa: College Placement Council, Inc., 1978.

Salmon, Richard D. *The Job Hunter's Guide to Eight Great American Cities.* Cambridge: Brattle Publications, 1978.

Standard and Poor's Register of Corporations, Directors and Executives Vol. 1. New York: Standard and Poor's Corporation, 1977.

The Executive's Corporate Handbook Joseph Lloyd Corporation. Winnetka, Ill.: Joseph Lloyd Corp., 1975.

Information:

Dun and Bradstreet, Inc., 666 Fifth Ave, New York, NY 10019. Publishes business directories.

Moody's Investors Service, Inc. 99 Church Street, New York, NY 10007. Publishes several manuals on business and industry.

II. *Christian Professions*
Information:

Christian Service Corps, 1509 16th Street N.W., Washington, D.C. 20000.

Intercristo, Box 9323, Seattle, WA 98109.

National Association of Evangelicals, 350 South Main Place, Carol Stream, IL 60187.

Yearbook of American and Canadian Churches 1977. New York: Abingdon Press, 1977. (Revised and published annually.)

III. *Education*
Directories:

Association of Christian Schools International, Directory. LaHabra, CA: ACSI, 1979.

Elliott, Norman F., ed. *Patterson's American Education.* Volume LXXIII. Mt. Prospect, Ill.: Educational Directories Inc., 1977.

National Union of Christian Schools, 865 28th Street Southeast, Grand Rapids, MI 49508.

State Offices of Education usually publish a directory.

IV. *Government Jobs*
Directories:

A Guide to Government Employment in the Midwest. St. Paul, Minn.: Midwest College Placement Council, 1976 (pamphlet).

Working for the USA. Washington, D.C.: U.S. Civil Service Commission, 1978 (pamphlet).

Information:

U.S. Civil Service Commission and Federal Job Information Center. See telephone directory under "U.S. Government" or obtain the toll-free number by calling 800/555-1212.

V. *Overseas Employment*
Information:

Opportunities Abroad for Teachers. Washington, D.C.: U.S. Department of Health, Education and Welfare, 1977-78.

Schultz, Gordon F. *How to Get a Job Overseas with an American Firm or Affiliate.* Burbank, Calif.: Overseas Employment Guides, 1977.

——————. *How to Get a Job Overseas with the United States Government.* Burbank, Calif.: Overseas Collegiate Research Institute, 1976.

VI. *Welfare and Service Agencies*
Directories:

Haimes, Norma, ed. Helping Others: *A Guide to Selected Social Service Agencies and Occupations.* New York: John Day Co., 1974.

Moore, Michele, ed. *Public Welfare Directory*, vol. 38. Washington, D.C.: American Public Welfare Assoc., 1977.

——————. *National Directory of Child Abuse Services and Information.* 1st ed. Chicago, Ill.: National Committee for Prevention of Child Abuse, 1974.

Information:

Local Welfare Office—inquire about state and local directories for organizations providing human services.

VII. *General Aids*
Directories:

Graduate and Professional School Opportunities for Minority Students. 6th ed. Princeton, N.J.: Educational Testing Service, 1975-77.

Graduate Programs and Admissions Manual 1977-1979. Princeton, N.J.: Educational Testing Service, 1977.

Renetzky, Alvin, ed. *Directory of Internships, Work Experience Programs and On-the-job Training Opportunities,* 1st ed. Thousand Oaks, Calif.: Ready Reference Press, 1976.

The College Handbook Index of Majors. New York: College Entrance Examination Board, 1977.

Information:

Encyclopedia of Associations, 10th ed., Vols. I and II. Detroit, Mich.: Gale Research Co., 1976.

Angel, Juvenal L. *Directory of Professional and Occupational Licensing in the United States.* New York: World Trade Academy Press, Inc., 1970.

Wasserman, Paul. *Encyclopedia of Business Information Sources.* 3rd ed. Detroit, Mich.: Gale Research Co., 1976.

APPENDIX E
Resources for Designing a Career Plan

Bachhuber, Thomas D. and Richard K. Hardwood. *Directions: A Guide to Career Planning.* Boston: Houghton Mifflin, 1978.

Bolles, Richard. *What Color Is Your Parachute?* Rev. ed. Berkeley, Calif.: Ten Speed Press, 1978.

Bradley, John D. *Christian Career Planning.* Portland, Oreg.: Multnomah Press, 1977.

Cull, John G. and Richard E. Hardy, eds. *Career Guidance for Black Adolescents.* Springfield, Ill.: Charles C. Thomas, 1975.

Greco, Benedetto. *How to Get the Job That's Right for You.* Homewood, Ill.: Dow Jones—Irwin, 1975.

Haldane, Bernard. *Career Satisfaction and Success: A Guide to Job Freedom.* New York: Amacom, 1972.

Jameson, Robert J. *The Professional Job Changing System.* Verona, N.J.: Performance Dynamics, Inc., 1976.

Knight, David M. *How to Interview for That Job—and Get It!* Connersville, Ind.: News-Examiner Company, Inc., 1976.

Looking Ahead to a Career. Washington, D.C.: U.S. Department of Labor, 1975 (pamphlet).

Pell, Arthur R. *The College Graduate Guide to Job Finding.* New York: Simon and Schuster, 1973.

Powell, C. Randall. *Career Planning and Placement Today.* 2nd ed. Dubuque, Iowa: Kendall/Hunt Publishing Company, 1978.

Reed, Jean, ed. *Résumés That Get Jobs.* New York: Arco Pub. Co. Inc., 1976.

Schein, Edgar H. *Career Dynamics: Matching Individual and Organizational Needs.* Reading, Mass.: Addison-Wesley Publishing Co., 1978.

Shingleton, John. *College to Career.* New York: McGraw-Hill Book Co., 1977.

White, Jerry & Marry. *Your Job: Survival or Satisfaction?* Grand Rapids, Mich.: Zondervan, 1977.

Guide Sheet — Column Headers (blank form, rotated)

Occupational Themes (p. 52): Realistic, Investigative, Artistic, Social, Enterprising, Conventional — R I A S E C

DOL Temperament Code (p. 51): Variety of Duties, Changes; Repetition, Standard Procedures; Specific Instructions; Planning, Being in Control; Dealing with People, Team Effort; Working Alone; Influencing People; Performing under Stress, Taking Risks; Sensory or Judgmental Criteria; Measurable or Verifiable Criteria; Interpretation, Personal Viewpoint; Precise Attainment of Standards; Dealing with Objects

DOL Work Values (p. 51): Business Activities; Routine-Concrete; Social Improvement; Reward of Prestige; Communication with People; Technical or Scientific Activities; Creative-Abstract; Technical Advances; Tangible Pay-Off

Adaptive Skills (p. 51): Conscientious; Dresses Appropriately; Enjoys Keeping Busy; Friendly; Relates Honesty; Objective, Sees Both Sides; Open to Change; Purposeful, Goal Directed; Resourceful, Creative Problem Solver; Respects Authority; Responsible; Accepts Self; Disciplined; Shows Empathy; Leads Wisely

Column numbers: 1 2 3 4 5 6 7 8 9 0 1 2 3 4 5 6 7 8 9 0 X Y 1 2 3 4 5 6 7 8 9 0 1 2 3 4 5 G V N S P Q K F M E C

DOL Aptitude Areas (p. 52): Intelligence, Verbal, Numerical, Spatial, Form Perception, Clerical Perception, Motor Coordination, Finger Dexterity, Manual Dexterity, Eye-Hand-Foot Coordination, Color Discrimination

H = Highly Skilled or Above Average
A = Average
M = Below Average or Least Skilled

SVP GED (p. 53): Educational Levels (see key below) — from, to

Guide for Selection of Potential Career Areas (Guide Sheet)

Once you have completed Steps 2 and 3 on pages 58-59, turn to appendix A, Chart 2. Chart 2 lists the worker traits that are associated with each of the sixty-six GOE career areas. Align the columns on this Guide sheet with the chart.

Look first at the Occupational Themes columns in the chart. Move this Guide sheet slowly down the chart watching for a match. Your best match is when your number-one theme appears as a capital letter and your second and third themes also appear (as either upper- or lower-case letters). If you need more matches or are just interested, your second-best match is when all three of your themes appear with your number-one theme in lower case. Finally, if needed, you may claim a weak match if any two of your three themes appear.

When you have a match, proceed to compare your profile of personal characteristics with those in the chart. When one of your arrows (↑) points to an x in the chart, circle the x. When there is an x in the chart but no arrow (↑) in your profile, mark a slash across the x.

Under Adaptive Skills, *only* circle x where you also have an arrow (↑). Having a match is very helpful but if you lack one or more adaptive skills it does not eliminate that career from consideration.

For the Aptitude Areas if a letter appears in the chart and this Guide sheet indicates an aptitude equal to or higher than that listed in the chart, circle the letter. If the chart calls for greater aptitude than you can claim, mark it with a slash; you may need to develop greater aptitude for careers in this group.

After making these comparisons, place an x by the WTG numbers on the back of this Guide sheet.

Now, continue to move this Guide sheet slowly down the page until you find the next match for your Occupational Themes and repeat the evaluation process just described. Proceed in this manner to the end of Chart 2.

Next, review the WTG numbers on the back of this Guide sheet. Are there numbers by which you placed checks (to indicate an association with your academic interests) that do not have an x? If so, use this Guide to do a comparison with these checked WTG numbers in Chart 2. Again use your "circles" and "slashes" to indicate the extent of agreement in the Occupational Themes columns.

Once your evaluations are completed, return to page 59, step 5, for further steps toward decision making.

Key: O = On-the-Job Training; H = High School; T = Technical or Two-Year School; C = College (4 years); G = Graduate School or Ten-year Apprentice.

WTG Numbers

01. Artistic
01.01 _____
01.02 _____
01.03 _____
01.04 _____
01.05 _____
01.06 _____
01.07 _____
01.08 _____

02. Scientific
02.01 _____
02.02 _____
02.03 _____
02.04 _____

03. Plants & Animals
03.01 _____
03.02 _____
03.03 _____
03.04 _____

04. Protective
04.01 _____
04.02 _____

05. Mechanical
05.01 _____
05.02 _____
05.03 _____
05.04 _____
05.05 _____
05.06 _____
05.07 _____
05.08 _____
05.09 _____
05.10 _____
05.11 _____
05.12 _____

06. Industrial
06.01 _____
06.02 _____
06.03 _____
06.04 _____

07. Detail
07.01 _____
07.02 _____
07.03 _____
07.04 _____
07.05 _____
07.06 _____
07.07 _____

08. Selling
08.01 _____
08.02 _____
08.03 _____

09. Accommodating
09.01 _____
09.02 _____
09.03 _____
09.04 _____
09.05 _____

10. Humanitarian
10.01 _____
10.02 _____
10.03 _____

11. Leading-Influencing
11.01 _____
11.02 _____
11.03 _____
11.04 _____
11.05 _____
11.06 _____
11.07 _____
11.08 _____
11.09 _____
11.10 _____
11.11 _____
11.12 _____

12. Physical Performing
12.01 _____
12.02 _____